SUCCESS

WRITTEN BY P.V

Billionaire tips to achieve anything you want in life...!

Copyright 2019 Paras Verma

All right reserved.

ISBN-20: 978-1-7986-17670

INDRODUCTION
SUCCESS

"Success is a journey not a destination. The doing is usually more important than the outcome."

Even the most common clichés contain a hint of truth. I often get stuck thinking about success as the end goal, so it's good to be reminded that success truly is a journey.

You know guys all the experience most of the billionaire gain in life is. Nothing will work unless you do; everybody is your friend until you ask them for a favor. So, there is only one way to do thing is don't depend on no one get thing done yourself because if you want to see yourself on the top position then just do what the 99% can't even think to do, if you want someone's expert advice in your life just talk yourself multiple times in front of the mirror coz it is the only thing that corrects you when you looking wrong, and please remember you're your own expert. Don't be sad because you're at a lower level of success remember great thing take time and you already see some of the examples in your home like just compare those luxury cars with your own family car you'll definitely see one of the biggest different easily. Just because it isn't happening right now doesn't mean it never will just have faith in yourself you can do it, just use those haters hate as a fuel of your success. Because you're never too old to follow your dreams whatever they may be, remember only one thing you are the only one who changes your life. No one can do it for you, and do a favor on yourself stop being so available for everyone all the damn time because that shows the weakness of your, being available for every is most dangerous disease of failure, I hope you remember those men's in suits look really successful but in reality they are working for the man in PAJAMAS.

You need to forget the mistake learn the lesson from it and do something new something that no one ever does in all those years because old ways won't open new doors just you need to remember these three words in life 'GOOD', 'BETTER', 'BEST'. Never let them the rest, till your good is better and better is best.

In this book, you will find some great facts that make you stronger and successful, and you have gone find some repeated point in the book because mean of success is repetition when you repeat things in life it will take you to near the success very soon with full of confident. And you know how to deal with every situation which comes to your path because you repeat thing in life; that's mean you are more confided then before. The points which repeated in this book are more common to whom who are near to the success.

Maybe some time thing gets tough than before it doesn't mean you can't do that; you can just focus on your goal because that's the only thing that makes you zero to something very soon; just believe you can and there is no one will stop you until you reach there.

Because you know; become zero to something you need to start today. Coz now or never is totally up to you so, now it's your call...!

P.V.

SHORT NOTE ABOUT

SUCCESS

THERE ARE TO ADVICE FOR YOU WHICH WILL YOU CHOSE

SOCIETY'S ADVICE	BILLIONAIRE'S ADVICE
Go to school	Go to school
Reads text books only	Also read self improvement books, like you already reading
Get a job	Start a business / startup whatever you want
Work 40 hours a week for a lifetime	Hustle for 80 hours a week for few years
Get married	Hire employees
Get in debt	Travel the word for new experiences
Work to pay off debt	Date a boss, marry a boss. you know what I mean
Have kids	Have boss children
Retire at age of 60	Retire at age 35
{DIE}	{LIVE}

HOW TO BE SUCCESSFUL IN LIFE?

THERE ARE 10 CHAPTERS THAT HELP YOU TO REACH THAT PATH AND 3 ADDITIONAL BUT MOST IMPORTANT ONCE...!

CHAPTERS

1. Think big..PAGE NO....- (01 TO 09)

2. Find what you love to do.......................................PAGE NO...- (10 TO 18)

3. Learn how to balance life......................................PAGE NO- ...(19 TO 40)

4. Do not be afraid of failure.....................................PAGE NO-... (41 TO 45)

5. Have an unwavering resolution to succeed......................PAGE NO..- (46 TO 47)

6. Be a person of action..PAGE NO..- (48 TO 56)

7. Avoid conflicts..PAGE NO...- (57 TO 63)

8. Don't be afraid of introducing new ideas.........................PAGE NO-.. (64 TO 68)

9. Believe in your capacity to succeed.....................PAGE NO...- (69 TO 79)

10. Always maintains a positive mental attitude................PAGE NO- ..(80 TO 87)

ADDITIONAL CHAPTERS BUT IMPORTANT

11. Don't let discouragement stop you from pressing on......PAGE NO-..... (88 TO 93)

12. Be willing to work hard..PAGE NO- ..(94 TO 99)

13. Be brave enough to follow your intuition........................PAGE NO..-. (100 TO 104)

"Let's start with first Chapter"

Think big.....!

1. THINK BIG.

How can we break through the limitations we've set for ourselves? That's what Michael Port, author of The Think Big Manifesto, wants to know. "Sometimes we assign the role of 'Big Thinker' to some people, but we don't necessarily see ourselves in that role," he says. Often, that's because of "voices of judgment" – either negative peers or colleagues telling you why something will never work, or (even more damaging) your own internalized voice, telling you the same thing.

But in order to truly thrive, he says, we have to let go of our self-imposed limitations – I can't talk to that person; she'll never hire me; that idea is too risky – and give things a try. Here are four of his best strategies to get going and expand your horizons now.

Get Comfortable with Discomfort. Port tries to practice what he preaches. When he was recently asked to give a speech to an audience of 3000 in Australia, he could have delivered a standard keynote address. Instead, he decided to hark back to his days as a professional actor and use the talk as an opportunity to develop an entirely new type of speech – a one-man show with music, film clips, and more. "I'm trying to do something I've never seen anyone do in a keynote before, ever, and if I pull it off, it'll be brilliant, and if not, I'll bomb, and there's not a lot in between," he says. "The best performers are the ones who take the biggest risks, and the performer who raises the stakes high enough is the one who is generally most compelling."

Set the Right Kind of Goals. Some believe that "thinking big" means you should set wildly ambitious stretch goals to inspire yourself to greater heights. Port doesn't buy that argument, however. "We sometimes set unrealistic goals for ourselves, and as a result, we're miserable," he says. "We're looking for a level so high, we can never be satisfied." He recalls the launch of his first book, the extremely popular Book Yourself Solid. "We started the launch at 9 a.m.," he recalls, "and by 11 a.m., it was the #3 bestselling books on Amazon. Then it went to #2 and stayed there for three days. It was behind Dr. Oz's book, which was on Oprah all week, and we were bummed because we weren't #1. That's because we had unrealistic expectations and I felt like I'd failed." Don't set yourself up for disappointment by setting ambiguously huge goals, says Port. Instead, "set a specific goal that's actually attainable."

Find Supportive Colleagues. Having a strong, positive peer network is crucial, he says. But that doesn't mean having a team of yes men. "There's a balance we need to find," he says. "Often, when we're asking people to support us, we're just asking for approval. But if we're looking for results, we have to be comfortable with the feedback of people asking us to think bigger." He cites his own example preparing for the talk in Australia. He invited a friend to critique his performance and she told him she didn't think the opening – which he'd spent 20 hours perfecting – didn't work. It was painful to hear, but ultimately helpful. "We think of supportive people as people who say yes. But if you're really looking for people to push you, you want them to say, 'That's great and I think you could improve this.'"

Become the Person Others Want to Help. "Other people determine whether or not we're successful," says Port. Thinking big requires understanding that the biggest and most meaningful projects simply can't be accomplished on your own. "Other people are going to open the doors and spread your messages." So how can you get others involved and inspired to help? It's all about attitude and reliability, he says. "You make commitments and fulfill them, you learn in action, and you deal with [your own] voices of judgment without being critical of others."

HOW TO THINK BIG

A lot of people say that thinking big is the key to accomplishing your biggest or most complicated goals, but it's hard to know where to start. Giving yourself some time to sit down and really think about what you want to accomplish is just the first part of thinking big. Creating a plan that you can follow up on, and staying motivated while you tackle your goals a little at a time can help you make a big thought a reality.

PART 1

USING YOUR IMAGINATION

1. Schedule thinking time.

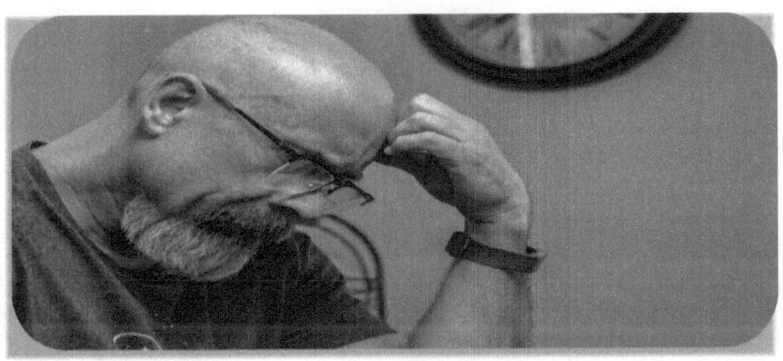

When you're ready to consider new projects or new approaches to current goals, set aside some time – 90 minutes, two hours, whatever you can spare – and use the entire time for thinking.

Using the whole time to think helps you come up with approaches and strategies you might not have thought of before, because we tend to come up with one or two good ideas and think "that's it! I'm ready!" Forcing yourself to think longer helps you go places your brain wouldn't ordinarily go.

Try to do your thinking in different settings. For example, you could go for a walk or visit a new coffee shop. Being in a different setting may help your brain to identify different possibilities than you would in your usual environment.

2. Entertain the impossible.

It's easy to think "small" in your life, because it's easy to feel obligated to be practical or realistic about your dreams or goals. Thinking big requires you to move beyond thinking realistically and toward what might seem improbable or even impossible.

For example, say you like to write. A realistic way of thinking about that might be to say that you want to write something every day. That's a realistic goal and a realistic way of thinking about your love of writing.

Entertaining the impossible means taking what you normally think you can do with your writing even further. Imagine what it would be like to see your book on a shelf at your favorite bookstore – maybe even in a fancy display. Imagine seeing your name and your book's title at the top of the New York Times Bestseller list. This is the easiest way to think big.

You can also do this by creating a vision board. Get a piece of poster board and use pictures and words from a magazine to represent your goals. Then, place the board somewhere you will see it often to help remind you of your goals.

3. Step outside your comfort zone.

Thinking big means thinking in ways that are beyond what you normally do, so naturally you'll have to step outside of your comfort zone. While you're thinking about new projects or approaches, let yourself feel a little uncomfortable. If you're not a little scared of what you're coming up with, you're not thinking big enough.

For example, if you have a speech project for school, but want to think big about it, consider giving a style of speech you're not usually comfortable with. Instead of reading directly from your paper, work from just a few bullet points and make it sound less formal. You could consider adding music or visuals to increase interest in your speech.

PART 2

SETTING GOLS

1. Set attainable goals.

Thinking big shouldn't also mean fantasizing about the impossible. It's tempting to set a wildly ambitious goal to try to inspire you to achieve something bigger, but doing so can be setting yourself up for failure.

For example, if you're thinking big about the kind of house you want to be able to afford one day, think bigger than you normally would – maybe $25,000 to $50,000 more, or a couple hundred thousand. But don't think so big that your plan is to be able to afford a home worth millions and millions of dollars. If one day you can, that's great, but setting more attainable goals helps to prevent you from being disappointed and helps you feel good about what you can accomplish.

2. Break up your goal in steps.

When you're putting your big dreams into practice, recognize that although your end goal is big – giving a speech, buying a house, publishing a bestselling book –

you have to take multiple, smaller steps to get there. The best way to achieve a big goal is therefore to break it up into smaller, more doable steps. Once you have your goal in mind, sit down and make a list of everything that you need to do for that goal to become a reality. This helps you to see it as more achievable and less overwhelming.

For example, if your end goal is to write a best-selling book, an example of starting small might be researching the topics or genres that are becoming more popular (you don't want to focus on stuff that's popular now, because chances are things will change before your book is finished).

If you're writing a speech, starting small might just mean making a list of things you want to give a speech about.

Once you have your goal broken down into steps, rearrange them in the order that you need to accomplish them.

3. Set deadlines for your goals.

Once you've established what your big goals are, you'll need to set deadlines for them. This makes you accountable and requires that work on accomplishing something everything day. It also helps to make all of the little steps you've created seem less overwhelming or more manageable.

Keep in mind that you may need to readjust some of your deadlines, so it is important to be flexible. Don't beat yourself up if some of your goals need to be readjusted.

4. Don't do it alone.

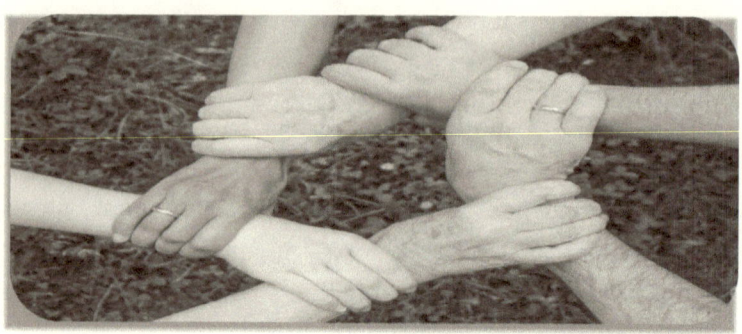

There's no way you can accomplish big goals all on your own. Bestseller authors don't publish, print, and distribute millions of copies of their books on their own. To determine what kind of people you need to help you achieve your goals, you'll need to do some soul searching to determine your own weaknesses. Are you unorganized? Are you easily distracted? Find someone to help you out who is a color-coding organizational guru. Ask a friend who has laser focus to help keep you focused on what you need to do.

Know when you'll need to use other people - like publishers or an agent, for example - to achieve your goals. Make sure you include contacting such people and whatever they need to do in your list of steps for achieving your goals.

5. Work consistently.

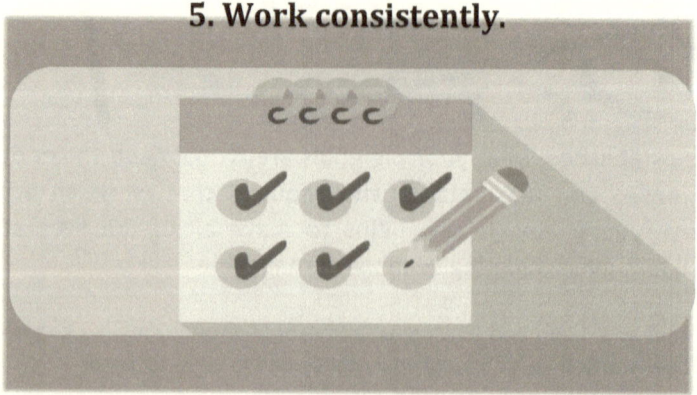

All of the thinking and planning in the world isn't going to matter if you don't eventually take action to make your big goal a reality. You need to work toward your goals every single day. It doesn't matter how slow you work or how long it takes to see results. If you work consistently toward a goal, eventually you're going to get there.

Creating a schedule for when in your day you work on each step toward your big goal can help you stay consistent. Set aside a certain amount of time each day – at the same time each day – to work. This prevents you from getting sidetracked by other things and guarantees that you stay consistent.

Remember that taking action doesn't necessarily mean accomplishing something really big every day. If you one of your steps for writing a best-selling book is getting an agent, don't get down on yourself if all you contribute toward accomplishing that step in one day is researching potential agents. You have to take the first step to take the second and as long as you're taking action, it doesn't matter how big or small the action is.

PART 3

STAYING MOTIVATED

1. Develop a support system.

The most important part of accomplishing big goals is realizing that you need the help and support of people who care about you. Having a support system in place can help you stay motivated. Surrounding yourself with supportive people doesn't mean surrounding yourself with people who will never critique your plans. You want people who will be honest with you and help you to improve your ideas.[9]

For example, if you're working on that speech for school, and you're committed to doing something different with it, ask a friend to listen to what you have and be honest about how they think it's going. It might be painful to hear that they think what you're trying just doesn't work, but it will ultimately make you better. And getting a new perspective helps you stay motivated.

You can also ask your support system to help keep you accountable. Share your deadlines or smaller step goals with them and ask them to check in with you.

Be careful of becoming overly reliant on others, too. If you spend too much time getting other people's opinions and following their suggestions, you'll get really good at helping them think big, but won't do so well thinking big for yourself. Criticism can be helpful sometimes, but it is important not to base your worth on what other people think. Relying too much on other people's opinions can be self-limiting.

2. Celebrate small victories.

It's easy to feel like you're not getting any closer to accomplishing your goals when you're focused on the little; everyday things you need to do to get there.

Celebrating small victories can help you feel like you are accomplishing something – because you are! – And keep up your motivation.

For example, if your goal is to have a best-selling book, you might celebrate the day you finish your research. Or the day you write a chapter. Or even when you get more than one page written in a sitting

You can celebrate in a lot of different ways, and they don't have to be expensive. Reward yourself with a piece of chocolate when you check off one of your steps. Or enjoy having a night off and binge a new TV show on a Saturday night. It doesn't really matter how you celebrate as long as you take a moment (or longer) to acknowledge that you're making progress.

Try placing a calendar on your wall and crossing off all of the goals you have accomplished, no matter how small.

3. Don't be afraid of failure.

If you focus too much on all the ways you might fail, or might fall short of your initial goal, you'll never have the motivation to get started. Everyone fails from time to time, and it's okay.[11]

Make a list of the ways that you might fail or fall short, and accept that they are distinct possibilities as you work to accomplish your big goals.

If you do fail, remember that your failure doesn't define you. Assess what led to your failure and start again.

Keep in mind that success is not a straight line from point A to point B. There will be challenges and setbacks along the way. Learn about some of the challenges you may face and consider how you will handle them.

"Now concentrate on second chapter"

"Second Chapter"

'Find what you love to do ...!'

2. FIND WHAT YOU LOVE TO DO.

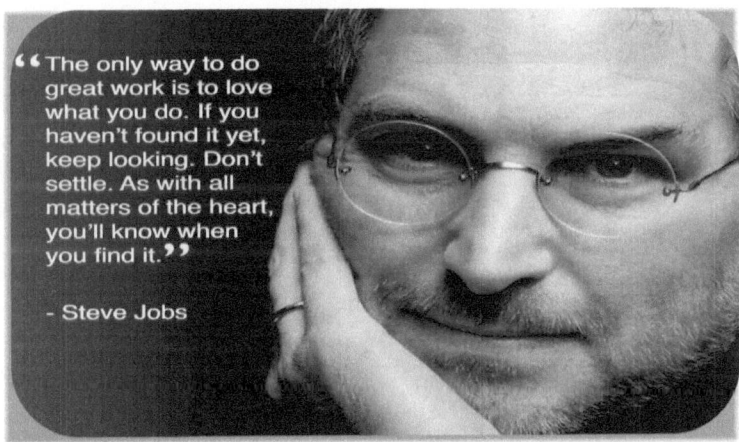

"Do what you love" is such a common bit of advice to young people trying to find their place in the world that one would expect it on a mug at your retired Aunt's house. It's become such a popular bit of advice that Silicon Valley contrarians and public personas pride themselves on offering the opposite advice (at least at first glance).

But it's easy to tell somebody to "follow your passion!" and "do what you love!" when it's just a platitude. If you're a young person trying to build your future, it can be hard to wrap your head around all the options in front of you. Even if you know what you enjoy, you probably don't know what you love, what you can do with what you enjoy, or how to put yourself in a position to do what you love. Even more, when somebody tells you "do what you love!" you can feel overwhelmed by all the options in front of you just for figuring out what you love.

You may enjoy fishing, but do you love it? How can you know? Compared to what? Maybe you love fishing compared to accounting, but maybe you would love graphic design compared to fishing. "Do what you love!" and "find your passion" only elicits "but how?" Unless you can try literally every job the world has to offer, you can never truly be sure that what you are doing is what you love.

We need some kind of way to sort out our options so we aren't stuck our entire lives trying to find a path.

Let's talk about the approaches; there are at least two approaches we can take.

POSITIVE APPROACH/ NEAGETIV APPROACH

POSITIVE APPROACH

The first approach involves trying everything and comparing experiences. This is what is described above. You try out different things and try to do more of what you like and less of what doesn't stack up.

I call this "the positive approach" because it is defined by doing new things. It implies positive action, adding things to a list as time goes on.

Maybe you feel contented while fishing, but excitement while flying. Maybe you feel excitement while flying, but euphoria while leading successful negotiations.

So, Negotiations > Flying > Fishing > everything else experienced so far.

Sound simple enough, right?

Not really….!

The problem with this approach is that there is so much not included in "everything else experienced so far." You can only experience so much in life, and even if you devoted ten years of your life to "finding yourself" and trying a "little bit of everything," there's a near-infinite set of permutations that you could experience, leading you on a chase to find that one thing you love more than anything else your entire lifetime.

To use the example immediately above, you may love negotiations compared to everything else, but this evaluation is entirely relative to everything else. Maybe you've never experienced software development, or the rush when you launch a new product, or skiing the Alps, or cobbling shoes with Nepalese monks.

This is the approach many young people are encouraged to take as they come of age. They're told college is a place to figure out what they love and try different things. They're encouraged to get a well-paying job so they can take vacations and try new things or have the leisure to explore themselves in their free time.

And it's no surprise when this advice is what's offered when you look at the approach to fulfillment embodied in the Baby Boomers and the generations raising young people today. Many Boomers and their peers took jobs that they didn't exactly love but didn't exactly hate, put money aside into a retirement fund, and then deferred their experiences for doing things they'd love doing until retired. It's only in retirement that they get to explore different options, though they've been trying their entire lives on the weekends, in college, and on vacations. With decades of searching under their belts, many are still left trying new things because the field "Everything else experienced thus far" is never all-inclusive in a world of scarcity of time and experience.

This is the story of the unfulfilled professional who works their entire life to get to do something they think they'd enjoy, only to find that it isn't that meaningful in the end. This is the story of the hedge fund analyst who loves basketball, gets the court-side seats, and only finds that it really wasn't worth all the work and is left trying to top the last experience. This is the story of most retirees. This is the story of the dopamine junkie. This is the story of the hedonic treadmill.

There is a better approach to narrowing down your options to do what you enjoy.

NEAGETIV APPROACH

If the positive approach is defined by trying new things and constantly comparing these experiences against each other to find out what you like more than other things, the negative approach is defined by eliminating things from your life.

Under the negative approach, we don't work towards trying more of what we relatively love and try to find more to make that "relatively" more accurate. We instead remove those things we don't like from our lives.

At first glance, this sounds like the same thing. If we do more of what we like, don't we automatically do less of what we don't like? If we do less of what we don't like, don't we automatically do more of what we like?

This may be the case, but the difference here is on where the mental focus lies.

If we are focused on finding what we love, we're on a perpetual search, moving up the hedonic treadmill as we compare more and more exotic and exciting experiences.

If we are focused on removing what we don't love, we're focused more on appreciating the options available to us. We indirectly guide ourselves closer to the things we end up really, truly enjoying.

HOW TO DO WHAT YOU LOVE

Whether you're a new professional or an experienced businessperson, working in a job you don't love can take a toll mentally. Your Sunday nights become filled with dread as you anticipate another day of watching the clock.

On the flip side, working in a profession you love can fill your life with joy and result in a willingness to work long weeks. Your dream job doesn't have to remain a fantasy.

FOLLOW THESE 10 TIPS TO DO WHAT YOU LOVE

1. Map out your GPS

(Greatness + Passions + Service)

When I first started trying to figure out how to find and do what I love for a living, I was confused just like everyone else. With so many ideas, it can be hard to pick just one thing. That's why I developed an exercise called The GPS Formula: the 'G' represents what you're great at. The 'P' represents what you're Passionate about. And the 'S' represents how you can provide a Service by combining both G+P.

The overlapping of the three (GPS) is your sweet spot for making a living doing what you love. Let's dive into the details of each individual portion of The GPS Formula so that you can discover a combination that's the right fit for you.

2. What are you great at

What are you great it? Seems like a pretty simple question, right? The unfortunate truth of the matter is, that most people have absolutely no idea how to answer it. Even worse; corporate cultures are predicated on trying to improve on weaknesses rather than cultivate strengths. And this puts a lot of us in an emotionally unstable position; making us feel as if we're not great enough or good enough.

So how do you figure it out for yourself? Make a list. Write down every single thing you're skilled at. When you're done with your list, you'll feel good about the fact that you've actually got something positive to look at on paper. Next, organize that list based on what you believe you're best at from the list of skills and qualities you've written down about yourself. Take your time with this.

3. Passion:

Don't try to find it. Try to bring it.

People get way too caught up in trying to "find their passion". Let me be crystal clear here – we do not find passion. Passion is a result. We bring it about by taking action.

We need to inject passion into the things we do. The best way to do that, is to try doing more of the things that you actually love to do. And while you're doing those things, you might find it beneficial to take note of whether you love that thing enough to try and make a living out of it.

4. Determine your highest point of Service.

Your highest point of service (or contribution) is where your greatest gifts (G) intersect with your passions (P) in a way that allows you to serve (S) other people. Similar to what I outlined for you above (see #3); this is where you focus on the "S" part of The GPS Formula — the part that requires you to produce value for other people (your employer, or your customers) so that you can actually make a living doing what you love.

The best way to figure out your highest point of service is to first make a list of the things you're great at (G), and second, to cross reference it with what you're passionate about (P). The third and final step is to figure out the best combination of G + P which will allow you to provide a service (S) so that you can make some moolah!

5. Always be reading.

People who do what they love for a living have a voracious appetite for learning as much as they can about the work they love to do. They're constantly looking for ways to expand their knowledge by reading the best books about their industry.

You should do the same. Once you've figured out what you love and want to do for a living, go find 5 of the best books about that industry and read them cover to cover. Or if you're on a time-crunch, And if you absolutely can't focus your eyes to text, try listening to the books in audio format.

6. Take action.

When I decided to start my own self-improvement podcast, I knew I needed to acquire some tech-related knowledge to get the ball rolling, so I took a course on how to start a podcast. The course taught me a lot of material, but I didn't wait until I was done with all 12 weeks of it to start taking action. No, no. Every single lesson was followed up with immediate action. Taking immediate action allowed me the opportunity to apply what I'd learned, and more importantly, to see if it actually worked. If I'd waited until the course was all over, I'd be overwhelmed and confused as to where to begin.

If you want to do what you love for a living, you need to always be taking deliberate action immediately after you learn something so that you can decipher the difference between what works and what doesn't.

7. Find a mentor.

It doesn't matter if you're learning from someone in real life, or if you're learning from them through their books and videos — find the best of the best in your industry and use them as guides and role models to help you become more successful and avoid painful pitfalls so that you can successfully arrive to that sweet spot where you'll be making a living doing what you love.

Wondering where — or how — to go about finding a mentor? Start by making a list of potential mentors. Next, learn more about them. Read their work. Follow them on twitter. Listen to their interviews. And if you've got the courage to do so, go ahead and reach out to them. They (probably) won't bite.

8. Get out of your comfort zone.

Several years ago, I used to be in terrible physical condition — fat, unhealthy, and totally out of shape. I knew that if I wanted to make a change, I'd have to get myself out of my comfort zone and dedicate myself to eating healthy and working out 5+ times per week. But I had my fair share of challenges. For example: It was scary to go to the gym because it felt like everyone was watching me and thinking "what's this worthless slob doing here..." But even though it was uncomfortable to go to the gym, I forced myself to do it anyway. Why? Because the temporary pain of feeling like people were watching and making fun of me, wasn't as heavy as the long-term pain I knew I'd feel if I didn't get a handle on my health.

Eventually, I got myself into the best shape of my life and developed a passion for health and fitness; in fact, I even ended up working as a male fashion model as a result. On top of that, my confidence improved and my energy shot through the roof! But I'm not telling you this to impress you, but rather to impress upon you, that it's crucial to get out of your comfort zone if you want to find and do what you love for a living, because the benefits of doing so will pour into every area of your life.

9. Don't burn yourself out.

A little grit never hurt anyone, but far too many folks hold the irrational belief that they must succumb themselves to back-breaking work in order to earn their keep. This is non-sense. Doing work you love isn't supposed to be totally easy. But that doesn't mean it's supposed to be excruciatingly hard either. People who do what they love for a living know that the secret to success is to cultivate a symbiotic relationship between labor and love. So remember: if you're burning yourself out, then you're doing it wrong.

10. Make friends with failure.

In order to successfully do what you love for a living, there's one thing you need to get comfortable with whether you're ready for it or not — failure. Throughout my own personal journey to doing meaningful work, I failed so many darn times I decided to create a public list of all my failures. This way, I can have something to look back on and learn from, and more importantly, something you and countless others can learn from as you embark on your own journey to doing work that matters.

If there's one thing I know for sure, it's that failure is inevitable on your path to success. But the beautiful thing about failure is that the more it happens, the closer you get to that sweet spot. That place you've defined as your own unique intersection of where your greatest gifts collide with your skills — coming together in a way that allows you to finally fulfill the dream that all of us are really after in life and business: to combine what we love to do with what we do for work.

"Now concentrate on third chapter"

"Third Chapter"

'Balance your life...!'

3. BALANCE YOUR LIFE.

Life, in many ways, is a balancing act — walking a tightrope and constantly juggling between work, home, money, health, and relationships. In a bid to accomplish our goals and to succeed on all fronts, we often fail to understand the importance of having balance in our lives.

Maintaining a well-balanced life isn't just crucial for your health, happiness, and well-being but also essential for boosting productivity, managing stress, and unleashing your true potential.

Most of us business leaders have a time in our lives when we just feel out of whack. Specifically, we feel like we've lost that sense of work-life balance. We know we may have been putting in too many 80-hour weeks in a row, and we can feel the side effects of making that kind of commitment. The crucial question then becomes: What are we going to do about it?

I've found that the best CEOs are always striving to find balance in their lives. That's what makes them great leaders and good people. And certainly we all need to put ourselves out of balance for a time, when, for example, we're in the middle of buying or selling a business. You know heading into that transaction that you're going to go out of balance. But the trick is to be conscious about that and know what you are sacrificing in the bargain. Then, once the deal is done, you should have a plan to get back into balance as quickly as possible.

So what are the secrets great CEOs use to live a balanced life? They measure themselves on seven key elements, where they give themselves a score from 1 (way out of balance) to 10 (Zen-like harmony) to see where they stand. I'm not sure I have ever met anyone who has scored a 10 on all seven elements, so a more reasonable goal might be to find balance with at least half of these parts of your life.

1. Physical health.

Whether you are a CEO or just a go-getter at work, it's easy to let things like exercise and diet go by the wayside once things get busy in the office. But that's the only body you're going to get and it needs to carry you until the end of the game. That's why it's critical to continue to keep your body strong and healthy enough to enable you to do the things that excite you-whether that's traveling for business or visiting your grandkids. The key here is to be fit enough that you don't have to say "no" to anything you want to do. Give yourself a score-be honest-and see what you think. Could you do more to improve that number as ways to begin leading the kind of balanced life you're seeking?

2. Family.

How balanced do you feel with your family time? What's your relationship like with your spouse? Your kids How about your parents and extended family members? Family ties are the tightest relationships you should have in your life no matter how busy things get at work. If you give yourself a low score here, it's worth hitting the pause button to make the investment in repairing these relationships. Family members are truly part of your support network and you'll never miss them more when you're at your lowest point.

3. Social.

Do you have a robust network of friends or not? Do you have a group of folks like you hang out with regularly, maybe for a book club or to go play soccer? If not, it's time to start building these kinds of relationships. Having people around you that you like and trust is one of the best indicators of living a long life. If you are sacrificing relationships like these because you're working too hard, you're clearly not in balance.

4. Financial.

What does your personal financial balance sheet look like? Are you on a path to accumulate enough wealth that you will be able to enjoy a comfortable retirement? Are your assets increasing over time-or have you neglected to make the time to tend your financial garden? The key to personal financial health is to feel in control and know that you have enough money to have options. If you're working too much, and you don't have the money you need, something is clearly missing in the equation.

5. Business.

Whether you are running your own business or climbing the corporate ladder, ask yourself how energized you are to go into work every day. Are you excited to be making a difference and making progress-or do you dread the monotony of your day-to-day drag? Or, if you own the business, how are things going: Are revenues and profits growing? Some of us who are high achievers might never give ourselves a 10 here no matter what. But it's worth measuring how all that time you are investing in your work is paying off.

6. Civic.

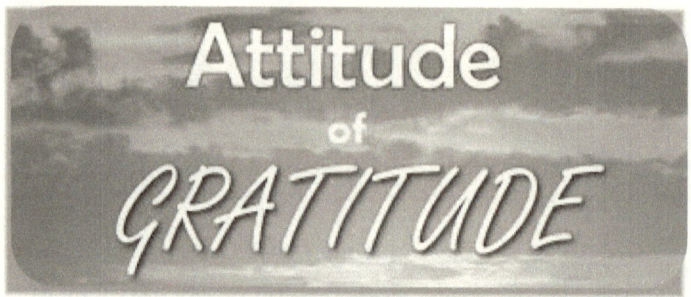

How much time are you able to invest in the things you care about in your community? That can mean anything from volunteering to serving on the PTA or coaching a sports team-anything that turns you on when you give of yourself. Think of it as your attitude of gratitude. If you haven't made enough time to give back, you're missing out on a real emotional payback, because you are rewarded by the act of giving. And the key here isn't just signing checks-time and talent is the real gifts.

7. Spiritual.

The final aspect of living a balanced life is your spiritual side. This could be anything from taking a walk in the woods to making a trip to church on Sunday- whatever fills up your spiritual cup. This is how we renew ourselves when we're down-and it's something that can be easily neglected. If you score low here, make the time to rethink your connection to God, nature, or whatever. You'll feel refreshed and ready to tackle the world.

LEARN HOW TO BALANCE YOUR LIFE STEP WISE

To start, what does it mean to be balanced?

To me, it means that you have a handle on the various elements in your life and don't feel that your heart or mind is being pulled too hard in any direction. More often than not, you feel calm, grounded, clear-headed, and motivated.

How do you find your balance?

The elements in life that require the most balancing can be divided into two categories: internal and external. Oftentimes, people focus on one more than the other.

For example, you may find that you focus on external things, like work, relationships, and activities, and that you pay very little attention to what is going on inside your heart and mind.

On the other hand, you may find that you spend so much time being self reflective that you sometimes misses out on the experience of living.

Other people may be fairly balanced between the two but might want to balance out some specific elements within each category; so I created this little outline to help us better understand the beneficial components on both ends of each spectrum.

Internal

(Mind, Heart, Health)

Mind:

Challenging yourself intellectually vs. creating opportunities for your mind to rest

Heart:

Giving love vs. receiving love

Health:

Eating, drinking, exercising properly vs. resting and treating yourself to some extra yummiest

External

(Work, Social, Family, Fun)

Work:

Pushing yourself to achieve goals vs. seeing the bigger picture and enjoying the ride

Social:

Satisfying your social desires vs. taking time for yourself

Family:

Fulfilling your familial responsibilities vs. creating healthy boundaries

Fun:

Allocating time for things you enjoy doing vs. making sure you don't overdo it

As you can see, both ends of each spectrum are actually positive; but if either side is taken to an extreme, something that is intended to be positive can end up being detrimental.

It's helpful to check in with yourself to see if you feel balanced.

Step first

Acknowledge

"Take some time to really look at your life, your state of mind, and how you're feeling. Be honest with yourself and notice the areas of your life that you're neglecting"

Until you reach the end of your dissertation there is always more work to do and the next action to complete. It is easy to focus on what you need to do or what you failed to do and forget to acknowledge yourself for what you accomplish along the way. Until you submit your dissertation for review, few people if any are aware of the day-to-day work you do or the times you pushed through and worked when you did not feel like it. There is no built in external reward system inspiring you to keep going. I believe an important strategy to sustain motivation over time is to pause and acknowledge yourself for what you do accomplish. No matter how much dissertation work remains, the small accomplishments along the way deserve to be acknowledged. Some students withhold acknowledgment from themselves because they believe that focusing on or even criticizing themselves for what they have not done or how much more there is to do will be more motivating. In my years as a dissertation coach, I have yet to see self-criticism or always focusing on how much more there is to do to be an effective long-term strategy for motivation and productivity. If those were effective motivation strategies, I would not have a job! When you pat yourself on the back and give yourself credit for your hard work, you are likely to feel more motivated and inspired to keep working. Acknowledgment of the work you do today increases the odds that you will look forward to feeling good for the future work you complete and be more present to your own capacity to get dissertation work done. Some of my clients actually write a statement such as, "acknowledge myself for a job well done" as the last action on their work plan for a given day or week as a reminder to celebrate their accomplishments. You deserve to feel good about yourself as you make progress on your dissertation. Stop, review your accomplishments at the end of the week, and acknowledge yourself for everything that you did accomplish. If acknowledging yourself feels awkward or uncomfortable at first, it is just a sign that you need more practice. In time, you will become more comfortable acknowledging yourself and come to see that celebrating your accomplishments is ultimately more motivating than dwelling in your failures.

Step second

Examine

"Notice if you're leaning more toward an internal or external focus or if there are areas within each category that you would like to be more balanced"

When we are out of line with Christian standards we have to ask ourselves, Am I a true Christian, or am I a counterfeit? Have I been born again, or am I only putting up a front? Those of us who are Christians ought to ask ourselves that occasionally. It is a good idea to examine you, especially if there is any kind of wrong behavior involved.

The very fact that the apostle could ask a question like that indicates that a possible answer is what marks true Christianity. A Christian, of course, is not simply one who joins a Christian church. Nor does adhering to a certain moral standard in your life or the fact that you consistently read the Bible make you a Christian. A true Christian is someone in whom Christ dwells. And the person in whom Christ dwells will have certain inescapable evidence of that fact given to him or her. Paul is suggesting that we ask ourselves if we have the evidence that Jesus Christ lives in us.

You may be asking, how can I know that? The answer is found in several places in Scripture. For instance, Scripture speaks of an inner witness. In Romans Paul says, The Spirit himself testifies with our spirit that we are God's children (Romans 8:16). That is one way you can know. There is an inner testimony, a feeling, a sense within produced by the Spirit of God who dwells within that you are part of the great family of God.

Scripture speaks also of desires that are born in the heart of a new Christian. First Peter 2:2 says, Like newborn babies, crave pure spiritual milk, so that by it you may grow up in your salvation. One of the marks of born-again believers is that they have a deep and sudden thirst for the Word of God, a hunger to be fed, to know the truth of God.

This inner change will also produce an outward change, which is not all subjective. We can answer the question, Is Jesus Christ in you? by observing our conduct, because the inner change will produce a different attitude toward our behavior. One of the striking things about new Christians is that they invariably begin to manifest a totally different attitude toward things they once thought were appropriate. In some of the more blatant forms of evil, such as attitudes about lying or drunkenness or stealing, they find immediately that their attitude is changed. That is because Christ lives in them, and light can have no part with darkness. Christ cannot share with Belial. Even our attitude toward our selfishness changes we see how selfish we have been. It looks ugly and distasteful in our eyes, and we want to be free from it....!

Step third

Set Goals

"Look at the outline to help you decide which ways you want to balance your life. Make a list"

Goals give a direction, a purpose, to everything that you do. Without them you are just aimlessly jumping from task to task and that can only lead to overwhelm, dissatisfaction and lack of success.

However, simply setting goals is not enough! You need to set the RIGHT goals for yourself.

If you ever wondered how to set goals the right way, this training is for you. It will show you the 3 must-haves of good goals (along with examples of goals) and how to avoid "fake" ones that waste your valuable time and energy.

If you want to be productive, if you want to be successful, you have to have goals. Goals give a direction to your life, give direction to what you're doing. If you don't have goals, you're just going, going, going, doing, doing, doing, 24/7, without really knowing why you're doing it and what are you trying to achieve.

But not all goals are created equal.

I find that a lot of people don't know how to set goals. They set goals that are either way too loose or way too narrow, or they set what I call "fake" goals. So I want to show you how to set the right goals, the right way. There is no bigger waste of your time than concentrating on the wrong activity.

HOW TO SET GOALS THE RIGHT WAY

1. Be Specific

First of all, a good goal is always specific.

You hear people say, "I want a bigger house. I want a new car. I want to be thinner, I want to be happier, I want my kids to be better."

That's not a goal.

That's a desire.

How do you transition from a desire to a goal? You make it specific.

What car do you want? What makes is it? How much does it cost? What house do you want? Where is it? What is it overlooking? Is it overlooking the ocean, is it overlooking a garden? How much do you want to lose in terms of weight? Is it 30 pounds, 50 pounds, 60 pounds?

Make it specific. That's how you go from a desire to a goal: making it specific.

Of course, you cannot attach a number to all your goals. Oftentimes, people want to be happier, and you cannot say "I want to be 3 points happier," because there is no way to measure happiness. If your goals are non-quantifiable, there is still a solution: try to add some sort of a point of reference. Say, "I want to be as happy as I was in college" or "I want to be as happy as I was 3 days before." Always add some sort of a reference so you know what you are aiming for.

If you don't know your starting point, your end point becomes blurry

2. Have a Deadline

A good goal also always has a deadline.

You want to lose 30 pounds by the end of the year. You want to buy your house by the time you're 35. You want to drive a new car by December 24th. Whatever it is, make it specific and add a deadline.

"Once you add a deadline to your goals, you schedule them. Once you schedule them, you make them possible"

Your mindset is going to switch into a different direction, because now you know you have a limited window of opportunity. Now you know your starting point. You know by when you need to achieve it. Even if it takes you 10 years, it's still a limited window of opportunity, and your mindset switches in a completely different way.

Always be specific, and always have a deadline. The goal setting formula is the following: you want to achieve X by Y.

3. Make Your Goals Positive

A good goal is also a positive one.

So many times, you hear people say, "Oh, I want to lose 30 pounds." That's specific. Good!

They might also say "I want to lose 30 pounds by the end of the year." That's a deadline. Even better!

Now, make it a positive one! Instead of "losing", try gaining. Try gaining energy, or vitality, or health. Try becoming healthier instead of losing weight. Instead of watching less TV, try spending more time with your kids, or more time at the gym, or more time walking outside. Instead of checking your email less, try to be more productive and concentrate more on the task at hand. Always try to switch the negative into a positive.

The great Oprah Winfrey says it best:

"If you concentrate on what you don't have, you will never, ever have enough"

Always turn the negative into a positive.

You're going to be happier, because when you concentrate on the positive, when you concentrate on gaining, earning more, expanding, instead of losing, cutting off, or contracting, your mindset changes. You start seeing the glass half full, instead of half empty which helps you keep motivated in the long run.

That's how you set good goals, the right way. Make your goals specific and positive. Add a deadline to the mix and you'll be on your way to achieving them.

But, here's the bad news: just because you have goals (even if you set them the right way), that does not mean they are the right goals for you.

Step fourth

Plan Tasks

"Make a list of daily, weekly, and monthly tasks that you will need to do to achieve each of these goals. What have you tried in the past? Did it work? If not, what can you do differently?"

As a small business owner your personal productivity can directly affect your company's success. Thorough planning can help you complete workplace tasks on time and to the best of your ability. Busy entrepreneurs can benefit from taking the time to plan tasks before diving in, whether the tasks be large or small, recurring or rare. Knowing how to plan a task at work can boost your personal productivity and heal.

1

State your objective in clear and measurable terms. Understand exactly what the end result of the task will be before taking the first step. Ask for clarification if you have been given a task that you do not fully understand, or if you have not been given all the details you need. Although business owners do not report to anyone directly at work, most tasks should have some stakeholder who can clarify task objectives. For example, if your task is to make sure that your new business is fully licensed and registered in your local area, contact the Secretary of State and County Clerk's office to clarify the exact requirements of the task.

2

List out or mentally note the resources, inputs and assistance required to complete the task. Realizing that you need additional resources once you have begun a task can slow down your progress, even grinding it to a halt if you have to wait for something or someone else. Analyze the potential pitfalls or challenges inherent in the task, and list out the resources you may need to have on hand to overcome these challenges. For example, if your task is to organize a conference call with your investors you will need to have information on all relevant parties' availability and you will need some sort of conferencing system in place that all parties will be able to use.

3

Determine the time constraints. First, determine whether your task is recurring or a one-time responsibility. If it is recurring, determine exactly how much time you have available to complete the task each time you do it. If it is a one-off, set a deadline for yourself to guide the rest of your planning.

4

Determine the time needed to obtain resources and complete the task. Simply preparing to begin a task can be just as time consuming as performing it. Preparation time will vary depending on the resource needs that you identified earlier. For the conference-call example, you may find that you need to set aside an hour to contact each of the stakeholders in turn, and that you may need to wait a day to hear back from one of the parties after leaving a voice message.

5

List out each step required to complete the task. This list can be a purely mental exercise for simple tasks; it can be a handwritten list for fairly complex tasks, or it might even be a detailed workflow diagram for highly complex tasks requiring multiple inputs from several sources. If your task is to obtain a local food sales license, for example, your steps may include obtaining an Employer ID Number from the IRS, downloading, printing, completing and submitting forms, scheduling on-site inspections and remitting payment to a local agency.

P you get more done in the limited time you have.

Step fifth

Reflect

"What is the most important thing you've accomplished in the past? How did you stay focused toward this goal? How did you handle your fears, doubts, anxieties, worries, and negative self-talk? How does it feel to know that you accomplished the goal in spite of these parts of yourself?"

"By three methods we may learn wisdom: first, by reflection, which is noblest; second, by imitation, which is easiest; and third, by experience, which is the most bitter."

For me Self-Reflection is the way to remove inner road-blocks, to first become aware of the things that really holding me back and then tackle them by finding a solution. Of course writing it down into a personal journal is the best way to do it. It's also interesting to do with a good friend who is open enough to take part. Some forms of psycho-therapy are similar to this approach, where you have a hopefully competent listener reflecting back to you and guiding you to a finally self-found solution.

This is a process of bringing inner road-blocks or wishes to the light are one of the most important things to do for personal inner growth. It's one of the best ways to attain clarity and by that immense power.

The alternative would be not making deeper personal issues conscious. If you do this you simply are not aware of them, maybe even denying them and by that saying ok to being limited. But they don't go away. They merely get stuck into the subconscious and then are influencing from there. Then you are polluting your inner space. Seen in this way, it is like not cleaning your room but simply looking away from your trash lying around; only that it is inner trash now. Having an inner cleaning mechanism is what Self-Reflection really is.

If you do this for the first time in such a depth you might feel a little bit weird, writing your own thoughts down and guiding yourself. I experienced this myself as I thought of this as weakness, to reflect on my problems. This is nothing more than social conditioning like "a real man (or woman) doesn't reflect on problems, he solves them". Of course this is totally stupid since analyzing a complex situation is the key to effective action and once I got the benefits of this process, I never gave it up again.

Step sixth

Prepare

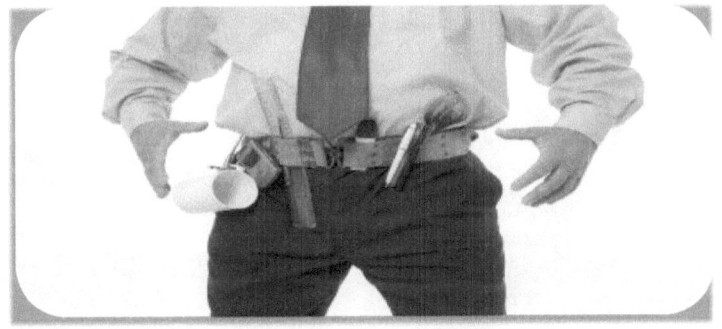

"Our inner "stuff" that will try to keep you from sticking to your plan (fears, worries, doubts, negative self talk)? Can you specify the things you will say to yourself to push you off track? (For example: "Just one more bite, I'll start eating better tomorrow") Make a list"

There are some pretty smart ways to be prepared for anything that happens in life, no matter how bad or unexpected it is.

Of course, you can't predict the future. Some people spend a lifetime trying to prepare for the worst. Sadly, what they end up doing is missing out on life today. They fear tomorrow, are always anxious about the next step of their journey and never stop to smell the roses and take a deep breath. That's not how life is supposed to be lived.

Instead, it's more about finding the balance between living in the moment and being ready for anything that can go wrong. I'll now show you some ways to do that strategically. All are different things you can try, skills you can build, or mindset shifts you can make. But the combination of these all will mean being able to deal with anything life throws at you in the future. While living fully in the present moment.

1. Let go of uncertainty.

First, let's develop the right mindset for this. The keyword here is acceptance. Meaning, accept that some things are out of your control they depend on outer factors.

Also, be okay with the ever-changing nature of life. It's what makes us learn and grow. Nothing wrong with it what you always have control over, though, is your reaction to external events.

Find peace of mind in the daily chaos. Once you do that, you won't get easily upset or angry. That's pretty useful as you'll then be able to clear your mind after something unexpected happens, and take a good decision.

2. Have your finances in order.

You can't move on if you're in dept. So let's begin with this when you finally get your finances under control. Regardless of how big the debt is or how long it might take you, do something today to begin the journey to financial freedom.

What can you do? Instead of feeling hopeless and spending even more on unnecessary things, sit down and write down the money aspect of your life plan. Break down the debt into smaller and smaller payments. Calculate what you can save money on in the next few months, so you can pay it off faster.

Once you're free, never get into debt again. Focus on saving after that. It's the foundation of building wealth too. When you know you have some money in the bank for rainy days, you'll sleep better at night. You'll never get to rely on somebody else to fix an unexpected expense too. That's another step towards freedom.

3. Learn how to survive.

The most important skill in life is to be adaptive. And for that, you need to test yourself in different environments and learn to survive. Then, nothing will ever bother you again in real life. We first need to make sure we're alive and doing well, before we move onto having better relationships or being healthier.

Most people today can only survive with the help of technology and the comforts of the modern lifestyle. But what happens when they get a flat tire in the middle of nowhere? Or need to change a bulb? Or see an old lady passing out on the street and realize they aren't sure what number to dial to call help?

These 3 examples are something you can Google and learn in a few minutes. Do it now. Then think of other basic things you might need one day. Learn how to do them in advance.

Not only would you be able to take better care of yourself and help others in need, but you'll also pick your brain. That will unleash your creativity and you'll suddenly start finding solutions to existing problems in your life.

4. Know what to do in case of an accident.

When facing a crisis or emergency of some kind, you need to take immediate action. Waiting can be crucial, be it for an injury or from a legal point of view.

What are you supposed to say when a policeman stops you due to drunk driving or being distracted and missing a sign? You might end up saying the wrong thing and making things worse.

What about having a car accident? It's key to take some necessary steps over the next few days to guarantee your safety. Speaking to an auto accident attorney is one thing on the list. You'll also need to prepare some information in advance though. And be able to answer some specific questions to have a valid claim. Ohio Valley PI Lawyers are one firm whose services will help you.

5. Have rough plans in mind.

Don't wait till the last minute to plan things out. I'm talking about short-term and long-term lists that you need to have, so that you follow the right direction and take decisions based on your end goal.

Could be a life plan, where you describe how you want each area of your life to look like some time from now. Then break each category down into goals, and then into specific steps. Now you can turn it into a 6-month plan to reaching a milestone.

Could be a business plan or your personal development plan Write your bucket list too. Or how about a list of things you should think about or get done over the next few months. No rush, just take a look at it every now and then to never forget something important.

Step seventh

Empower

"What do you need to remember in those times? What are things you can say to that self-sabotaging part of yourself? Be kind to yourself. Balance won't feel good if you're cruel to yourself in creating it"

There are many possible reasons - you work for a boss that you hate but you just can't quit, you want to start a business but you just can't think of a great idea, you want to get married but you just can't seem to get a date, etc.

Powerless people have one thing in common - they love to use the word "can't". They've used it so often that they don't even notice it anymore but "can't" is a dangerous word.

When "can't" is used, all progress and creativity stops. You are declaring that there is no other solution and that's the way it's going to be.

What's interesting about "can't" is that it doesn't really mean anything on its own. It's merely a shortcut for three possible meanings:

I Don't Want to...

"I can't go to the concert tonight." = "I don't want to go to the concert tonight; I would rather stay home and relax."

I Don't Know How...

"I can't speak Russian." = "I don't know how to speak Russian."

I Don't Believe Me Can...

"I can't lose weight." = "Even though I know the method for losing weight and I want to lose it, I don't believe I can lose weight.

Before you read on, test this out. Think of a time when you used "can't" and see if it fits one of those three meanings.

"Surprised?"

I definitely was. I still remember how excited I was when I tested out the different times I used "can't" and realized it really did fit one of the three meanings.

From that point on, I became aware of my usage of "can't" and began replacing it with the real meaning. I use to think "I can't build my own website. I don't know anything about html or programming." but when I realized what I really meant was "I don't know how to build a website.", it made it clear why I wasn't where I want to be and that I can do something about it. I truly felt empowered. My website and blog are the results of this empowerment.

If you're not where you want to be, ask yourself why not? If your answer contains "can't", is it because you don't want to, you don't know how to or you don't believe you can.

If you don't want to, then that's fine because that's your choice.

If you don't know how, you can choose to learn.

The easiest one of the three to overcome is if you don't believe you can because all you have to do is change your belief which takes about one second and can be done without getting up from your chair.

There you have it with some time to spare. Remove "can't" from your vocabulary today and get ready to make some real progress in your goals and in your life by turning your dreams into possibilities.

Step eight
Connect

"Is there a person or a tactic you can use to keep yourself supported, motivated, and focused in those hard times? I highly recommend connecting and sharing your inner process with someone. Find someone who can help you challenge your inner demons, and celebrate your little accomplishments"

One big mistake people make is not realizing that happiness is an individual choice. But every choice is influenced by the people in our lives. If you change your life influencers for the better, you can dramatically increase your chances for happiness and success.

In my research, I've found that positive social connection is the greatest predictor of long-term happiness. Welcoming a positive new influencer into your world can be one of the most important choices for happiness you make. That person might be a professional life coach or a mentor or simply someone whom you respect and who has the positive outlook you want to emulate.

A positive influencer will have a few outstanding traits that rub off on you over time. This person will practice gratitude. He will seek joy daily and work at becoming his best self. He'll enjoy being active and feel connected to others.

Think about the negative influences around you. These are people who focus on the bad things in their lives and cause you to do the same. You'll be left searching for new problems to worry over. Negative influencers don't smile or laugh easily. They have trouble maintaining relationships and see stress as a threat rather than a challenge to embrace. Steer clear!

We know that happiness is a choice. But we continually need to be reminded by people to make that choice, especially when life gets challenging. Think about the people you know who could be positive influencers and spend more time with someone who will improve your happiness and lead you to greater success.

Step ninth

Plan

"Just like accomplishing any goal in life, it takes time and effort to overcome your habitual patterns and create new ones. If you stay on track with this detailed and intentional process for three whole months, then there is a good chance you will create new habits to enjoy a more balanced life going forward"

Have you ever tried to plan something and just gotten completely overwhelmed? Today, I'm going to give you my PAT formula for planning anything—along with the one tool I use to make any planning process dead simple.

I'll dig into the details of the PAT formula in just a minute. But first, the thing I love the most about the PAT formula is it's applicable to just about anything you might be planning. Maybe you're building a business, or writing a book. Maybe you're creating something smaller, like a podcast episode or a blog post. Or maybe you're planning an event, like a party or a vacation. It could even be something as big as a wedding.

Whatever it is, planning it the right way is really important. Smart planning helps ensure that your event or book comes out great, by providing a clear roadmap to completion. The problem lies in the way our brains work. You see, our brains do a really good job of coming up with a bunch of ideas, but a terrible job of organizing them. And as a result, we get overwhelmed.

THAT'S WHAT THE PAT FORMULA IS

So what is this magic formula that helps you avoid the overwhelm It involves three steps:

Step 1:

Post-it notes

Step 2:

Arranging those Post-it notes

Step 3:

Taking it and making it

"You can be better prepared for almost anything in life. What do you think?"

"Now concentrate on fourth chapter"

"Fourth Chapter"

'Do not be afraid of failure...!'

4. DO NOT BE AFRAID OF FAILURE.

The third block in the second tier of Coach Wooden's Pyramid of Success is Initiative. He chose to direct his definition of this trait at the individual by urging him or her to "cultivate the ability to make decisions and think alone. Do not be afraid of failure, but learn from it."

Coach Wooden's college coach at Purdue, Piggy Lambert, once inspired Coach with these words: "The team that makes the most mistakes usually wins." He was emphasizing that it is the doers who make mistakes. This was an important lesson in shaping Coach Wooden's teaching philosophy.

Coach wanted mistakes of commission, not of omission or of carelessness. In other words, he wanted his team to be made up of doers. "We must not be afraid to act," he said. "If we are afraid to do something for fear of making a mistake, we will not do anything at all. That is the worst mistake of all. You learn through adversity. We get stronger through adversity." Coach firmly believed that if you were not making any mistakes, you were not working close enough to the edge of your potential.

One of Coach's favorite poems was a short verse that embraced exactly this concept:

When I look back, it seems to me,

That all the grief that had to be,

Left me when the pain was o'er,

Stronger than I was before

Coach Wooden once described the needed behaviors and leaders the same behaviors and character traits of a great parent. "We must not be afraid to fail," he insisted. "We, as parents, I think, deprive our children, the ones we love the most and want to help the most, of the development of initiative by making decisions for them too long in certain areas…. Lincoln said: 'The worst thing a parent could do for his children is doing things that they could and should do for themselves.' Give them the opportunity to fail. Let them learn from it so that they won't make that same mistake again when you are not there telling them what or what not to do. Initiative will help us overcome many stumbling blocks."

The same lesson is, of course, applicable to a teacher or coach or mentor—anyone in a position of leadership. Coach often reminded us that if we make a decision based on careful planning while using all the information available to us at the time and act with self-control, but it doesn't lead to the results we'd hoped for, that doesn't mean we made a bad decision. It just means it's a decision that didn't work out. The result should not discourage us from taking initiative in the future.

HOW TO DO NOT BE AFRAID OF FAILURE

Fear of failure is a significant obstacle that stands between you and your goals. But it doesn't have to be.

Fear of failure is the intense worry you experience when you imagine all the horrible things that could happen if you failed to achieve a goal. The intense worry increases the odds of holding back or giving up. Being successful relies to a large extent on your ability to leverage fear.

What can you do to prevent fear of failure from setting you back?

1. Redefine failure as discrepancy

Success is often hard to define. Failure is even harder.

What is your definition of failure? Giving up? Never going after your goals? Not achieving a desired outcome? Not achieving the desired outcome within an expected timeline? You may think that the answer to this question is obvious. But it is important to be clear about what you consider failure, since failure is the object of your fear and the obstacle to your success.

To make your goal pursuit fail-proof, switch from thinking about failures to thinking about discrepancies between what you hope to achieve and what you might achieve. Discrepancies provide you with information that you can study, explain, and learn from so you can recalibrate your future efforts.

As long as you continue making effort, there is no room for failure. When you give up altogether, for no better reason than fear of failing, that's a different story!

2. Distinguish between real and imagined threats

Fear is our response to two kinds of threats: real and imagined. You already know the difference. Real threats pose a risk to our survival. Imagined threats are hypothetical scenarios. Delivering a speech in front of a group of people is an imagined threat because there is little risk to your survival. Delivering a speech in front of a pride of lions in the savanna is a real threat because they are not interested in hearing you, they are interested in eating you.

Fear of failure by definition involves imagined threats. And while the fear is real, the threat is not. For the time being, the threat is a prediction, a product of your imagination, a scenario you built. This doesn't make your fear unfounded or irrational. But it makes it premature and unnecessary. Instead of letting it stop you, study it and plan how to avoid the consequences you're scared of.

3. Create promotion rather than prevention goals

The research on goal achievement suggests that there are two types of approaches that people take with respect to their goals: approach and avoidance. I like to call them promotion and prevention goals.

Promotion goals are about achieving a positive outcome (e.g., "I want to get a raise," "I want to expand my client base," or "I want to get a promotion"), while prevention goals are about avoiding a negative outcome (e.g., "I don't want to lose my job" or "I hope I don't get a negative review"). Prevention goals are associated with more disorganized approaches to goal pursuit, lower engagement, less self-determination, and more anxiety. Moreover, prevention goals lead to the creation of more prevention goals in the future.

Fear of failure leads to the creation of prevention goals, which may blur our focus, undermine our efforts, and make planning difficult. Reframing prevention goals as promotion goals is one way to take fear of failure out of the equation.

While most of us set promotion goals at one time and prevention goals at another, it is important to remember that how we frame our goals can obscure our intentions, delay implementation, and make it easier to give up.

4. Expect a good outcome but do not become attached to it

The more attached you are to the outcome you envisioned when you set the goal, the more likely it is that you will interpret discrepancies from that desired outcome as failure. As circumstances change and as your experience changes you, what you initially saw as the ideal outcome may no longer be attainable, appropriate, or meaningful. However, if you choose not to re-evaluate or adjust the outcomes you expected, you will be stuck in discrepancy and convinced that you are failing. The research shows that people who reappraise their goals and are able to adjust either their approach or their expectations enjoy better physical and mental health.

Some goals require focus and persistence. Others, however, require openness and flexibility. Being able to reevaluate and redefine the outcome you hope to achieve is a good buffer against fear of failure. We should evaluate our success by the amount of thought and effort we put forth, rather than by the outcome we achieved.

5. You are strong and you can prevail

Fear of failure is not about the challenges ahead or the effort required. It is about the consequences we may suffer if we fail. We are not afraid of the work we have to do, but of the remote chance that our work will not be good enough to yield results that meet our standards.

Researchers on fear of failure have identified several negative consequences people with fear of failure expect, including feelings of shame and embarrassment, a big-blow to self-esteem, the prospect of an uncertain future, the loss of social influence, and disappointing important others (more on this topic here). Notice that people estimate the psychological cost of failing to be much higher than the material cost. People with fear of failure are less worried about losing money than about losing friends, losing face, or losing faith.

To attenuate fear of failure further, identify the consequences of failing that scare you the most and evaluate your ability to deal with these consequences. Instead of talking yourself out of the fear by hoping that nothing negative would happen, focus on building confidence to deal with the consequences.

"Now concentrate on fifth chapter"

"Fifth Chapter"

'Have an unwavering resolution to succeed...!'

5. HAVE AN UNWAVERING RESOLUTION TO SUCCEED.

No matter how old you are, where you're from or what you do for a living, we all share something in common—a desire to be successful. Each person's definition of success is different, however, as some may define success as being a loving and faithful spouse or a caring and responsible parent, while most people would equate success with wealth, fame, and power. We all want to achieve success so we could live a comfortable life—have financial freedom, drive a nice car, and live in a beautiful house. However, although success can be achieved, it does not come easy. I think there is an immutable conflict at work in life and in business, a constant battle between peace and chaos. Neither can be mastered, but both can be influenced. How you go about that is the key to success. But sometime if you do fail, it I simply the opportunity to begin again but this time more intelligently I have accomplished a lot of things, many people do but they do not sat back and let things happen to them. I think we went out and happened to things. But sometimes it happens that u has a great idea, but the truth is your new idea is crank until the idea succeeds. So, fight for it. And it is very important to dream, you do not have to rich to daydream. Also try to push yourself further than you could have imagined, then only u can cut out for the top position.

From Colonel Sanders, Founder of KFC:

"I made a resolve then that I was going to amount to something if I could. And no hours, nor amount of labor, nor amount of money would deter me from giving the best that there was in me. And I have done that ever since, and I win by it. I know."

This, in many ways relates to the above quote about learning from your failures.

It's the easiest thing in the world to give up from a failure. The only way to push on is if you have the true burning desire to succeed, to not be moved or dissuaded from your goals.

If you are not truly dedicated towards success, then each failure will hurt more, each set back will slow you down.

Success is hard; without the unwavering desire to succeed, this difficulty may seem insurmountable. With the desire, it is merely an obstacle to go through.

"Now concentrate on sixth chapter"

"Sixth Chapter"

'Be a person of action...!'

6. BE A PERSON OF ACTION.

Do you sometimes feel stuck and unable to take action?

I do.

To get what you want out of life you can't sit around wishing for it to happen. And wishing that someone else will do it for you don't work too well either.

In this article I'd like to share 4 simple habits that help me when I get stuck in inaction and that have worked very well for me to go from a lazy guy who spent too much time on the sofa watching TV to becoming a focused and effective person of action.

Start your day in the right way

How I start my day has probably become the most important factor for how much action I take during the day and how the day turns out in general. A good start often leads to a good day. A bad or indecisive start often leads to a pretty mediocre day.

So create a morning routine with breakfast, perhaps a short work out or a short meditation and other things you find gets you off to a great start.

Then add doing the most important task of your day at the end of that morning routine. That usually works well for me to build a productive day where I take quite a bit of important action.

On some mornings I may feel low in energy, unmotivated or have extra inner resistance to taking action. Then I start small instead of starting with the most important task.

I do maybe some decluttering or clean up a bit. I may do a deal with myself to just work for 5 minutes on a relatively easy task. Or if that feels like too much I make a deal with myself for 2 minutes of work. The most important thing is that I get started and get moving. If I do that then I will continue to keep moving forward.

Break down it down into small steps

Work can become overwhelming and filled with negative feelings when you look at a big project or task.

You want to escape. You procrastinate. Then you become stressed because there is a deadline somewhere down the road and you are giving yourself less and less times to complete this thing as you procrastinate.

A big help here is to form the habit of breaking down big things into small, manageable steps that you can have done pretty quickly today and that will not give you anxiety or pump you full of negative emotions.

So break down a task into small, practical steps that there is an end to. If you have to read a book then breaks that task down into reading for 30 minutes. After you have read for 30 minutes check this off of your to-do list or just tell yourself that this task is done.

In my experience, it is very important to feel that you have finished tasks at the end of your day and to not have them hanging over you as you go home, spend the evening trying to relax and as you go to bed. Your mind wants to know that a step is finished – even if it is a small step like reading for 30 minutes – to be able to relax fully and to not create vague stress inside of you.

So break it down into small steps. Look at and focus on just that first step single-mindedly until it is done. Then continue to the next step and focus on just that. Do that and you'll waste less extra energy on worrying and on your work?

Celebrate what you did today.

This is something I am still working on and something I can do more of. But it makes a big difference when I do it. You have to appreciate your good work to feel even better about your life and yourself.

So take two minutes out at the end of the day to think about what you can appreciate about what you did today. Or write down a couple of self-appreciative things in your journal. Have a tasty treat or a bigger celebration. Tell someone how nice something turned out or how proud you are over something important you did today.

Reward yourself for the things you did right today to strengthen your action taking habit. And remember to be kind to yourself for the things you may have missed or not gotten done. No point in trying to beat yourself up. No point in trying to be perfect. See what you can learn from it and perhaps try another solution tomorrow instead and see if that works better.

Take one small action right away to get the ball rolling.

What is one thing you can do to pretty much make sure that something will get stuck your I'll-do-that-when-I-have-the-time list for a long time?

Read about something and get excited about it. And then do nothing about or tell yourself that you will take action tomorrow.

Instead, take one small action today, as soon after you have read about whatever you are excited about. Call up your friend and make arrangements to meet this Sunday night at seven to start working out, trying yoga or eating at the new restaurant.

If there is an exercise you can do in whatever you read about and it looks promising then does it today. If that feels hard make a deal with yourself to only work on it for 5 minutes.

If you want to travel somewhere in particular then don't stop at a vague dream. Take a few minutes and look up prices online and then look at your budget and see how much you need to save or earn extra to be able to take that try.

HOW TO BE A PERSON OF ACTION

1. Stop waiting for ideal conditions

If you wait until conditions become ideal, you'll probably never start working. Almost always there will be something that will stop you. Either time an appointment is not suitable or market crashed, or excessively large competition in place. In this world there is no perfect time to start a business. You have to act and solve problems. The best time was last year. Second chance is right now.

2. Be a man of action

Train yourself in performing and acting rather than thinking your steps over. Trying to start to do sports? Need to talk to your boss about performance? Do it now. The longer lives an idea in mind, the weaker it becomes. After two or three days, the details begin to blur. A week later you forget your idea. Becoming a man of action, you will be able to do more and stimulate the emergence of fresh ideas.

3. Remember that ideas alone do not bring success

Ideas are important, although they become something substantial only when they are implemented. 1 implemented idea is worth a dozen of the smartest ideas whose owners are waiting for the best time to start. If you have an idea that you really believe in, do something. When you start you won't escape.

4. Use action to frighten your fears

Have you ever noticed that the most difficult part of taking a public speech is actually waiting for your turn? All professional speakers and artists feel the same excitement before performance or speech. As soon as they start talking, excitement disappears. Action is the best way to frighten your fear. The hardest thing to act is to take the first step and do something first time. As you start, you gain confidence and it becomes easier and easier to keep on going Eliminate fear by taking action and build on the success of confidence

5. Start your creativity mechanism automatically

One of the worst misinterpretations of the creative process is that you should start working only when inspiration comes. If you wait until inspiration does not fall on your head you will act fairly infrequently and with long intervals. Instead of waiting for inspiration start working and creativity will come along. If you need to write something then takes a pen and start doing that. Your brain will switch on the creativity mechanism as soon as you will start doing something.

6. Live in your present

Focus on what you can do now. Do not worry about what you should have done last week or what you will do tomorrow. The only time that you can change is now. Even if you think about yesterday or tomorrow you can't act in those times.

7. Act immediately

Usually people prefer to have a small talk before business meetings. The same happens to those who work alone. How often do you check your mailbox and Facebook before you start serious work? These distractions will cost you dearly if you do not learn to ignore them and get to work immediately. Starting to work immediately you will find out within yourself fresh sources of productivity see you as a leader and great manager of your own resources.

You need to be a very organized person to get down to business without the help of others, without a command from the above. This is probably why right motivation is the key. In companies managers have to find the right motivation for the employees to start and keep them concentrated on working. Do not miss the wave of your motivation. Acting people are always noticeable either for themselves when they have things done or for the managers in the companies by seeing them as high performers.

STOP OVER THINKING SO MUCH & GET INTO ACTION:

Many people constantly over think about what they want to do but then they don't take action because 'fear of failure' overtakes them. Thinking too much stops people from taking action. People have thoughts of failure and they see the worst possible outcome. It seems as though many have a negativity bias, the mind of many has become tainted by illusions of not succeeding. The key is to stop over thinking so much and just get into action straight away.

But the thing to understand is that failure is not failure, most people think failure is bad, when in actual fact, failure is only feedback of what you need to improve upon. Disassociate failure with not being good enough, as the ones who fail fast and improve upon their previous attempts are the ones who make progress at a more rapid rate.

Take action, stop thinking too much. Get out there and get into action. Those who do are the ones who get to know themselves truly, but the ones who do not do not ever get to know the person they could have been.

Take Action Straight Away:

Many people like to deliberate about what they want they do, it is great to plan and then take action but many a time people spend many hours planning but never do anything to see what works and what doesn't

Take action straight away in all aspects of your life. Just do it, Nike's slogan is so true, just do it and see what you are capable of, make it a habit to take action as soon as an idea or opportunity presents itself.

Each day we are presented with opportunities of growth if only we would grasp them, the opportunities of growth help strengthen us within ourselves, don't just let life pass you by wondering what could have been, the best way to know is to take action straight away.

Get Serious About Success:

Once you decide to get truly serious about success in all areas of your life then that is when true change takes place. Your level of dedication and commitment to success will push you to take action. When you make up in your mind that you are serious about becoming a successful individual you develop this sense of urgency within to act, to make progress, and to make things happen.

Fear Disappears With Action:

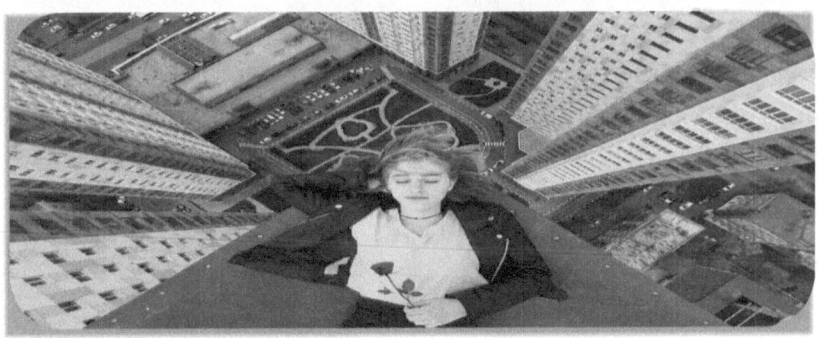

Fear is a false state of mind that many have allowed to cripple them in their pursuit of a greater life. But if you take action, fear disappears and you are able to see more clearly, your sight is sharpened and your mind is strengthened. Never allow fear to hold you back, attack the things that you fear valiantly and you will start to become the person that you want to be.

It is important that you surround yourself with action takers, people who are going places and doing something with their life. As the people whom you spend the most time with you will become like them. You need to distance yourself from the ones who don't take action and ignore their views on success. Don't let the cowards and timid folk of the world make you like them, it takes nothing to be average.

If you are in the company of those who challenge you to raise your game and believe in you then you will be inspired and motivated to take action.

Daily Action Taking:

Allocate time daily to taking action in all aspects of your life. Make it a routine, a daily success routine of taking action so that you make forward strides in the attainment of your goals. By taking action daily you will build up momentum on the path of success and that will help you to become the action orientated individual that you want to be.

Action Makes All The Difference:

Your life will never ever change or improve if you do not take action. Let's just cut out the nonsense, you can read as many success books as you want, you can talk about your dreams as much as you want, you can dream up some great dreams, you can watch all the motivation videos you want, you can attend all the success seminars in the world, you can do all the online success courses, you can have the right beliefs, attitude, ambition, mindset, and mentality for success, but nothing will ever move you forward unless you take action. Action is the key. Action is what makes all the difference.

Conclusion:

Time waits for no one to courage up, be the person you see, be the person that you know deep down inside of yourself that you know you can be, not tomorrow, not next week, month, or year, but today, be an action taker and make your dreams a reality.

"Now concentrate on seventh chapter"

"Seventh Chapter"

'Avoid conflicts...!'

7. AVOID CONFLICTS.

Conflict avoidance is a method of reacting to conflict, which attempts to avoid directly confronting the issue at hand. Methods of doing this can include changing the subject, putting off a discussion until later, or simply not bringing up the subject of contention. Conflict prevention can be used as a temporary measure to buy time or as permanent means of disposing of a matter. The latter may be indistinguishable from simple acquiescence to the other party, to the extent that the person avoiding the conflict subordinates their own wishes to the party with whom they have the conflict. However, conflict prevention can also take the form of withdrawing from the relationship. Thus, avoidance scenarios can be either win-lose, lose-lose or possibly even win-win, if terminating the relationship is the best method of solving the problem.

The term "conflict avoidance" is sometimes used to describe conflict prevention. Bacall criticizes this use of terms by asking,

Is there a difference between preventing contracting AIDS by the use of appropriate precautions, and avoiding or not seeking treatment if one has contracted it? Of course there is

Turner and Weed classify concealment as one of the three main types of responses to conflict, describing congealers as those who take no risk and so say nothing, concealing their views and feelings. Congealers are further divided into three types; namely:

Feeling-swallowers who swallow their feelings they smile even if the situation is causing them pain and distress. They behave thus because they consider the approval of other people important and feel that it would be dangerous to affront them by revealing their true feelings.

Subject-changers who find the real issue too difficult to handle they change the topic by finding something on which there can be some agreement with the conflicting party. According to Turner and Weed, this response style usually does not solve the problem; instead, it can create problems for the people who use this and for the organization in which such people are working.

Avoiders who go out of their way to avoid conflicts

HOW TO AVOID THE CONFLICT

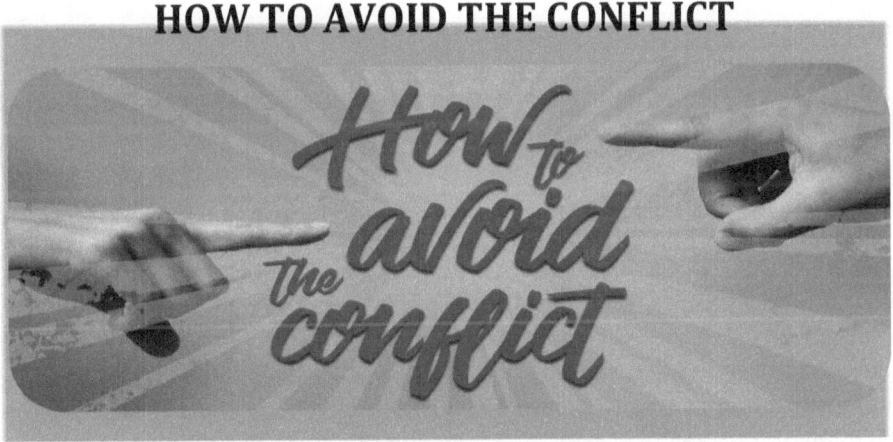

A difference in the opinions, values, understandings and thought processes of individuals lead to a conflict. When individuals strongly oppose each other's ideas and concepts, a conflict starts. It has been observed that when people think in dissimilar ways and are not willing to compromise at all, conflict arises.

Conflict can start anytime and at any place when individuals are not ready to accept the middle path approach. A conflict results in verbal arguments, abuses, and tensions and also spoils relationships.

Before starting any conflict one should take some time out to think, "How will this fight benefit me?" "Is it going to provide me any solution?"

Nothing beneficial and productive comes out of a conflict. It is simply wastage of time and energy for and thus every individual should try his level best to prevent conflict.

First learn to keep a control on your emotions. Never ever get too hyper or overreact as it leads you nowhere. Always remember the other individual you are dealing with might not be as educated as you, might not be from the same background as you are, but you have no right to ridicule his opinions. Be a good and a patient listener. Listen carefully what the other person has to say and then only give your expert comments. Even if you don't agree to his suggestions, don't just start fighting, instead discuss with him. Both of the individuals must try to compromise to some extent and find a solution. Conflicts only add on to your anxiety and thus it must be avoided at any cost. Never be rigid on any point, instead be flexible and try to find out an alternative.

Learn to keep a control on your tongue. One must think before he speaks. Don't unnecessarily shout on others as it not only spoils the ambience but also brings a lot of negativity around. Soften your voice while interacting with others and learn to adjust with others. Sit with the other person and try to sort out your differences.

Misunderstandings also lead to conflicts, so be very clear and transparent in your communications. Never play with words and the content of your communication has to be specific to avoid conflicts. Do cross check with the speaker whether he has understood everything in the desired form or not, failing which would lead to misunderstandings and eventually to a fight. Effective communication goes a long way in preventing conflicts. Don't always expect the other person to understand everything on his own. It is your moral responsibility to make him aware of what you exactly expect out of him.

Every individual has the right to express his views and opinions, and you have no right to criticize him. If you respect other individuals, you will get respect in return. If a conflict arises among group members; make sure you address all the participants together. The issues and problems must be addressed on an open forum. Personal favors and biases must be avoided for a peaceful environment. Listen to each and everyone's opinion and then only take a decision. Be a good leader and try to take everyone along. Keep your mind calm and composed.

Don't feel guilty if you have done anything wrong, instead admit it. Never hesitate to accept your faults. Be the first one to apologize. A small sorry can work wonders and prevent conflicts and unnecessary tensions.

If the other individual is too demanding and adamant and is just not willing to listen, the best solution is to avoid him. You can't be everyone's favorite, learn to ignore people who are just not flexible and always ready to initiate a conflict. Don't always bother what the other person has to say about you. Always act in a manner which you think is appropriate and don't just blindly trust the rumor mills.

No one wins in a fight and you gain nothing out of it. As they say "Prevention is better than cure", thus a conflict must be prevented at its early stages as it snatches one's mental peace and harmony.

There are some steps which you can apply in your life to avoid conflict.

1.

Understand the underlying reasons for conflict in the workplace. Emotion often gets in the way of sensible resolutions. People may feel angry at unreasonable situations, which leads to stress and explosions. If they have unresolved anger issues, they may avoid conflict until resentment boils over. Individuals lacking confidence act out constantly in their attempts to always be right or get the one-up In some cases, greed leads people to focus on their own needs and go to any means necessary to get what they want. Jealousy, anxiety and insecurity also lead to conflict in the workplace.

2.

Be realistic in your goals. The closer the relationships and the more opportunities there are for conflict, the more trivial complaints become significant ones and the more intense the feelings. Some conflict in the workplace is inevitable, so it's important that you learn how to minimize conflict. Understand that sources of satisfaction or conflict include: love, status, service, information, goods, money and shared time. Seek to balance these factors as best you can to avoid conflict.

3.

Assess your attitude to see if you are programmed to avoid conflict. You need to believe the following: A mutually acceptable solution is possible. A mutually acceptable solution is desirable. Cooperation is better than competition.

Everyone is of equal value. Other people have legitimate views too. Differences in opinion can be helpful. Coworkers are trustworthy. The other party can compete, but will choose to cooperate.

4.

De-escalate your peers' anger. Conflict doesn't come out of nowhere. Often it begins with an angry comment. Over time, the perception that a person's feelings are ignored or devalued leads to explosive conflict. Keep attune to what's going on around you. If someone is angry, respond compassionately by acknowledging their feelings and finding points of agreement. If the anger is directed at you, a sincere apology is always disarming.

5.

Arrange a mediation session. If conflict seems inevitable and tensions run high, scheduling mediation with an impartial third party is the best way to avoid future conflicts. The mediator will set the tone by providing a brief introduction and deciding upon the goals for the session. Each party will then tell their side of the story, being careful to avoid blame. The mediator will attempt to define and restate the problem to better articulate the source of aggravation. Both parties will be asked for solutions and a satisfactory agreement will be reached by all.

6.

Assess your communication style. If you find yourself always embroiled in conflict with others, the problem may be what you're saying or how you're saying it. Avoid person-centered statements that begin with "You never," "You always" or "I hate it when you." Keep your comments focused on the present moment, rather than rehashing the past. Avoid manipulative attempts to make the other person feel guilty or asset blame. Steer clear of making unsolicited advice or lengthy attempts to persuade someone. Never use language that incites anger, such as swear words, racially insensitive lingo or terse phrases that include "whatever."

"Now concentrate on eight chapter"

"Eight Chapter"

'Don't be afraid of showing new ideas...!'

8. DON'T BE AFRAID OF SHOWING NEW IDEAS.

It's a dilemma so many entrepreneurs face: Taking you great idea public now, when the market seems ready, or wait until you have patented or otherwise protected your intellectual property. Then you ask, is the cost worth it? How long will it take?

These are the same questions Allison Krongard asked herself when starting her company, WallCandy Arts. She started the company around the development of her unique, reusable wall stickers and wall art – products she's named Wall Candy. Having been in the design business for many years, she came to her product idea after being asked by several friends and family for ideas to decorate their children's rooms. "I treated their children just like clients, trying to determine what they liked and wanted. But I soon learned that each time I'd meet with them, their preferences has completely changed. As someone who didn't have children at the time, it was eye-opening to see how fast their tastes change and grow. So I wanted to find a way to create a design that could change with them."

Allison launched her company in 2001 by exhibiting at trade shows, where, she admits, there are pluses and minuses. "By exhibiting at the trade shows, you can become an international company overnight. Your product will be seen by all the buyers – but also by everyone who is going to try to copy your ideas. My products have been copied, but as a former boss once told me, 'If you keep your secrets, you'll never sell them.'"

After seeing her WallCandy being copied, she decided to file a patent on a newer product – a peel-and-stick, removable, reusable chalkboard. Still waiting for the patent after almost four years, Allison said, "The 'patent-pending' designation is only obeyed by the truly ethical, so going out with that means you still have to be willing to risk being copied. When the patent comes through, you can ask them to stop, but by that time, who knows how much money they've made." In her case, a larger competitor made a bid to buy her company. After opening up her company – and her products – to their due diligence, they then backed away from the sale. Then they produced their own identical chalkboard product.

"That was really hard to see, especially since I know they're making millions off of that product. I'm a small company, so what am I going to do? Spend all my money litigating, or spend my money innovating? As friend of mine said, when a larger furniture company stole his chair design: 'Prada doesn't care what Dockers is doing they're both selling pants.' So I see that being copied is just confirmation that my idea is good, and I have to put faith in my creativity. They can't take that from me."

I asked her what she's doing to differentiate WallCandy against competitors and imitators, and she told me that she uses a more personal approach to marketing: "On my Web site, I incorporate room ideas to help my customers figure out how to best use the product in their home. I've also introduced new products that extend beyond décor, such as a peel-and-stick whiteboard (in addition to the chalkboard) and two designs called Monster Patrol and Smarts, one intended as a tool for parents to help their children deal with fears of the dark and the other created with images to help stimulate newborn cognitive development. There are also customers' photos as well as photos of how I use the product in my own home to help inspire even more ideas."

Allison continues to invest in developing new products, despite the copycats stealing some of her business. And, she doubled her revenue not only last year but nearly every year since she launched.

Don't be Afraid to share ideas with anyone

Personally recommendation by the billionaires

In my lifetime, I might have got numerous amazing ideas. Some might have worked or some might not. Not all have been implemented and very less have been shared amongst my friends and even to the strangers. I couldn't apply each of them because it was not possible for me to do all of them by myself, circumstances weren't favorable and mostly It didn't fall into my priority list. But the strange part is, having known that I won't be able to pursue all of them, I didn't share all to the people nearby either.

Why I didn't share them is an interesting question. The first of all is: being scared of having the idea copied and not being credited for that. Second is: I was busy counting the chicken before they hatched. And the third is: I didn't understand ideas that came to me, came to me free; greed overcame me.

In order to understand the ideas we need to observe how they came to us. Ideas are merely the combination of the information that we obtained from various sources and media. They just fitted perfectly at one time and the bulb in our head glow. This means that we didn't create anything new but we just fused the knowledge we had and brought a solution to issues we came across. So, do we actually need to put the value in it? I believe not. There is no need to be possessive about it. Ideas come and go, most of them are forgotten too, until we see or hear someone applying it. At that moment, we might frown a little bit for self not being the implementer. We might get amazed to see a person thousands of miles away doing it and we hadn't shared about the idea to anyone. While saying that, there is still a light but significant contentment in seeing that the idea worked, and this needs to be our focus. We need to consider it as a natural phenomenon in which an inspiration flows.

Hence, we should not get disheartened to see our ideas being copied by one to whom we shared it. Had we kept it in our grasp, neither would we let the seed (idea) grow into a tree though any action nor would be able to move on. The greed holds us back and ghost of unborn ideas would haunt us. This wouldn't only limit ourselves to the ideas which might have been significant in that moment; we also close doors to other possibilities.

If the great thinkers in ancient times were obsessed about their ideas, the development and evolution wouldn't have been possible. Due to the advancement in the sharing of knowledge and ideas, innovations have been sprouting in every moment. They are so short-lived that new upgrade can be observed. For example, nowadays big companies are competing in the market not just to take time in doing research but also bringing their product as soon as possible in the market. This is because every single time they get late, competitors might introduce early and they might get hard time to sell the products.

The idea of 'Idea' is to putting it in action and taste the fruit. And if it's not possible, then it's wise enough to share or broadcast it to as bigger audience as possible. Let the inspiration flow unabruptly and witness our idea grow with or without our recognition. It's because inspiration is the feeding for the innovations and change. Let's care, share and grow together. Let's contribute happily in the evolution for the better future,

"Now concentrate on ninth chapter"

"Ninth Chapter"

'Believe in your capacity to succeed…!'

9. Believe in your capacity to succeed.

Self-image is not the same as conceit or an overinflated ego. It is, instead, a genuine self-respect, a positive mental picture of yourself that grows out of the recognition of your untapped potential. Unless you can develop a strong self-image, you greatly diminish your chances for success in personal leadership. Your self-image sets up an invisible barrier. You set your own ceiling and cannot rise above it or progress beyond it. Unconsciously, you mark a line and say, "Beyond this point I cannot go."

If your self-image is negative, every decision filters through a network of unconscious fears and doubts. If you think that you are worth very little, that your talents and abilities are limited, you will unconsciously refuse to achieve very much. Ironically, the world is filled with people who have every attribute for personal leadership except self-confidence. They rate themselves so harshly that their low self-image relegates them to the ranks of plodders who venture little and gain less.

Although you cannot rise above it, you can raise your self-image. If you believe, "I can," you are correct. If you believe, "I cannot," you are also absolutely correct. It is a simple psychological fact that you act like the person you believe you are.

If you view yourself as a failure, you will fail no matter how hard you consciously try to succeed. You may accidentally outstrip your self-image for a time, but you will quickly readjust. We see an example of this on the professional golf tour. There are a dozen or more professional golfers who earn a comfortable living, yet never win a tournament. Often they lead by five or six strokes for the first two or three days of play but then manage to adjust to their self-image. You sometimes hear them tell a sports announcer something like this: "I have really been playing over my head," or "I don't believe how far ahead I am." Quite predictably, they adjust to their self-image and shoot enough bogies to lose the lead. They never win first place because their self-image is a fraction too low.

A low self-image produces negative attitudes that hamper development of personal leadership by forcing you forever to grapple with internal fears and doubts. If you cannot respect yourself, you cannot in turn, respect others; and if you cannot respect yourself, neither can others respect you.

One difficulty in maintaining a positive self-image is that most of us have been taught that self-love is wrong. Perhaps this is rooted in a misunderstanding of humility and in the idea that self-love is equal to selfishness. Nothing is further from the truth. We are told to love our neighbors as ourselves — not more than ourselves, nor instead of ourselves, but as ourselves. You must have respect for yourself. You need make no excuse for doing so.

Because the exercise of personal leadership springs directly from a strong self-image, you must learn to appreciate your potential and develop a self-image equal to the importance of the role you play in life. It would be futile, however, to attempt to use the external facade of positive thinking to substitute for a positive self-image.

How then can you go about improving your self-image? You must redirect your thinking and alter your attitude about yourself. Learn to appreciate and respect your own importance. You are the most elaborate machine ever designed. Your potential is unlimited.

You are unique in all creation; nowhere on earth is there another like you. There is never a basis for a comparison of one person with another, but by a process of growth and unfolding, you can make a contribution that no one else can duplicate. Knowledge of your personal strength and worth can help you to build a strong bulwark of security within your heart.

"Motivating Yourself"

You cannot wait for someone else to head you in the right direction; you must motivate yourself. Motivation is an inner need or drive that impels or incites an individual to action. Motivation is a desire held in expectation with the belief that it will be realized. Belief comes from your self-image, expectation comes from your reserve potential, and any desire supported by belief and expectation becomes a strong motivating force that propels you toward your goals. Self-motivation is neither a mystical power nor a gift that descends from the heavens by chance. It grows, blooms, and flowers. It finds expression when you prepare for it, attract it, and reach out to receive it.

Human desires, needs and drives are fairly universal; but goals and behavior are individual. Two people may behave in diametrically opposite ways to reach identical goals. It's important for you to understand the universal drives that influence your actions, and learn to set goals and direct your actions toward achieving them.

How to believe in your capacity to succeed step by step with the help of book author

Step first:

Ask God to increase your capacity.

1 {Chronicles 4:10 in the Amplified Bible says :}

"Jabez cried [prayed] to the God of Israel, saying, oh, that you would bless me and enlarge my border, and that your hand might be with me, and you would keep me from evil so it might not hurt me! And God granted his request."

Have you ever asked God to increase your borders . . . you capacity for a greater blessing flow?

I'd like to believe that most of you have. However, the real question is . . . did you ask in faith believing . . . not wavering or doubting?

I've known way too many believers whose faith comes in sudden bursts . . . when their back is against the wall or even when it's convenient.

When we ask God . . . we've got to know that He is a rewarded of them that diligently seek Him.

Step second:

Charge out of your comfort zone by challenging the way things are.

Stretch your thinking. . .increase your understanding. . .do something you've never done. . .enlarge your capacity for increase by believing something. . .you previously thought impossible.

Believe God . . . like Abraham who left what was familiar and held onto the promises of God.

Believe God . . . like Noah who had never seen rain but built the ark.

Believe God . . . like the Centurion who knew one word from Jesus would bring life to a dead situation.

Believe God . . . like David who took a rock and rolled the giant.

If God is going to enlarge your borders you'll need to leave your comfort zone and the predictable behind so He can increase your capacity to believe and receive beyond your previous expectations.

{Genesis 12:1-2 in the Amplified Bible says :}

"Now [in Haran] the Lord said to Abram, Go for yourself [for your own advantage] away from your country, from your relatives and your father's house, to the land that I will show you.

"2 And I will make of you a great nation, and I will bless you [with abundant increase of favors] and make your name famous and distinguished, and you will be a blessing [dispensing good to others]."

Step third:
Put on your spiritual glasses.

We must stopping looking at life through our rearview mirror . . . at what's happened or didn't happen in the past.

Our future is in front of us . . . and we need to allow the Word of God to be the glasses through which we view our capacity for success. We need to see the world before us through the promises of the Word.

To increase our capacity for success . . . our blessing flow . . . we need to have 20/20 vision.

2. {Chronicles 20:20 says :}

". . . Jehoshaphat stood and said, Hear me, O Judah, and ye inhabitants of Jerusalem; Believe in the Lord your God, so shall ye be established; believe his prophets, so shall ye prosper."

To believe the Lord our God . . . is to see things as He sees them. Take a moment to allow that statement to sink in...He is the God of limitless possibilities.

Step fourth:

The miracle of thinking big . . . likes God.

LET GO & LET GOD.

Years ago, I read a book entitled "The Magic of Thinking Big" by David J. Schwartz. It's a good book. . .but truthfully, I'm not into magic. . .I'm into miracles. . .the supernatural intervention of God to change circumstances. Miracles Come When You Think Big and Don't Doubt.

When our thoughts line up with His thoughts and they should . . . because 1 {Corinthians 2:16 in the Amplified Bible says :}

"For who has known or understood the mind (the counsels and purposes) of the Lord so as to guide and instruct Him and give Him knowledge But we have the mind of Christ (the Messiah) and do hold the thoughts (feelings and purposes) of His heart."

{Colossians 3:16 in the Amplified Bible says}

"Let the word [spoken by] Christ (the Messiah) have its home [in your hearts and minds] and dwell in you in [all its] richness, as you teach and admonish and train one another in all insight and intelligence and wisdom [in spiritual things, and as you sing] psalms and hymns and spiritual songs, making melody to God with [His] grace in your hearts."

{Now that's how we expand our capacity for success and His blessing flow}

Step fifth:

Negative conversations will adversely affect our capacity for increase.

We can never be motivated by those who aren't motivated.

We can never share dreams with those who aren't dreamers.

We can't talk about achieving our goals with those who don't have any.

If we desire to increase our capacity . . . we need to make sure we hang around the folks who can help fill that capacity with the pure, the powerful and the positive from God.

People who will cause us to stretch our thinking while expanding our borders.

1 {Corinthians 15:33 in the Amplified Bible says :}

"Do not be so deceived and misled! Evil companionships (communion, associations) corrupt and deprave good manners and morals and character."

Step sixth:

Positive associations will dramatically increase our capacity for success.

Make it your business to learn from people who've been or are at where you want to go.

In selecting a mentor . . . here are three things you should consider.

First, does your mentor have the proper spiritual insight to train you?

Second, has your mentor actually experienced the advice they are giving you?

Third, does your mentor have a successful track record in the area in which they're advising . . . be it the marketplace or ministry?

Advice that has not been tested, proven and successful is just opinion . . . an experiment … not experience.

Someone, regardless of how good they sound,. . . cannot take you where they haven't been.

When it comes to your capacity for success and change . . . you need to realize that every new generation can go beyond the previous generation.

{Proverbs 15:22 in the New Living Translation says:"

"Plans go wrong for lack of advice; many advisers bring success."

Step seventh:

No one can limit or restrict your capacity for success . . . unless you allow them to do so.

Enlarge your tent . . . the place of your surroundings. Make and take conscious decisions to move beyond past limitations.

According to the Herring Life Experiences Dictionary . . . breakthrough is defined as:

"A sudden burst of faith that will take you beyond all previous points of past resistance."

In other words, you . . . nobody else but you . . . will make a decision to move beyond the boundaries that societal inertia or attacks of the enemy have taken you.

May your capacity for success be commensurate with the blessing flow that God is bringing into your life . . . beginning today.

{Psalm 40:5-7 in the Amplified Bible says :}

"5 Many, O Lord my God, are the wonderful works which you have done, and your thoughts toward us; no one can compare with you! If I should declare and speak of them, they are too many to be numbered.

6 Sacrifice and offering you do not desire, nor have you delight in them; you have given me the capacity to hear and obey [Your law, a more valuable service than] burnt offerings and sin offerings [which] you do not require.

7 Then said I, Behold, I come; in the volume of the book it is written of me;"

Some bonus tips by the billionaires

No matter what you do with your life - whether you go to college or fine tune your craft; build a business or climb the corporate ladder; get married or sail through the world solo - some people will support you, while others will criticize your choices and doubt your ability to succeed.

"You can choose to listen to the skeptics, or hit the ignore button," says career coach Michael Peggs. "Walking around with a 'Do Not Disturb' sign may seem like the answer, but it's a Band-Aid solution. People will continue to judge, criticize, and discourage you. Let them."

Let's talk about important tips

Talk to the "man in the mirror."

You are your own worst critic, Peggs says. "Too often we look in the mirror, skip what's right, and focus on what's wrong." Believe in yourself first, and others will follow suit.

Remain positive and confident.

"We all studied Isaac Newton's third law of motion in school: for every action there is an equal and opposite reaction," Peggs says. "Do good and good will come to you."

He says attitude is everything - but positivity alone will never produce progress. "In fact, your slips and falls may strengthen your skeptics," he says. "But keep in mind that a diamond cannot be polished without friction, nor a man perfected without trials."

Hear your haters, but pay them no mind.

"Hate is a by-product of fear, and it will call your name at the most vulnerable of moments," Peggs explains. "Take a message. It's not what you're called; it's what you answer to that matter."

Pay less attention to what people say, and focus on why they're saying it. "What is their motivation? Is it to lift you up or put you down? Inspire or deflate?" Actions speak louder than words, and people will always show you who they are.

Get back up after every fall.

When you're attempting to accomplish something, you'll make mistakes - and mistakes might look like failure in the eyes of your skeptics. "Never mind that," Peggs says. "Keep going. Success is a journey, not a destination, and you will grow along the way."

Give them a reason to believe in you.

Show your skeptics you can succeed; don't just tell them. "Too often we talk a big game," Peggs says. "But you need to give people a real reason to believe you can succeed."

Success takes time, and the path is always longer than it looks. "So be persistent."

Don't surround yourself with too many skeptics.

Some criticism and skepticism is healthy - but too much can be detrimental to your success. You need to be surrounded by fewer doubters than supporters.

"And just remember that by overcoming obstacles and facing skeptics, we're able to rise above and be better than we were before," Peggs concludes.

"Now concentrate on tenth chapter"

"Tenth Chapter"

'Always maintain a positive mental attitude…!'

10. ALWAYS MAINTAIN A POSITIVE MENTAL ATTITUDE.

That's about 80% of all of your thoughts. The vast majority of our thoughts are unpleasant, stressful, or self-sabotaging. Our brains are like a network news channel, only reporting the bad stuff with a sprinkling of good news to keep us from throwing ourselves off a cliff.

I'm sorry if this information just added to your negative thoughts, but hopefully the awareness of how steeped we are in negative thinking will give you pause.

Negative thinking is almost always focused on two areas — the past and the future. You ruminate and relive painful, frustrating, or shameful past events, or you fret about some anticipated event or encounter that hasn't happened.

Either way, you're tethered to an illusion. The past is gone. The future doesn't exist. But somehow you're able to create a tremendous amount of discomfort over these non-existent scenarios. Your thoughts run rampant in your brain, creating all sorts of havoc without anyone stopping them. It's like having a toddler in the house whose parents implement no rules or restrictions.

Here are some best ways to create a positive attitude:

1. Create awareness.

Put a rubber band on your wrist as a reminder to notice your thoughts. When you look at the rubber band, take note of your thoughts and feelings. Sometimes you can catch yourself in the middle of a rumination or worry. Other times you might notice you feel anxious, irritated, or sad, but you aren't immediately sure why. When this happens, ask yourself what the thoughts are that have produced these feelings. By paying attention this way, you'll see how often you get caught up in negative thinking.

2. Break the spell.

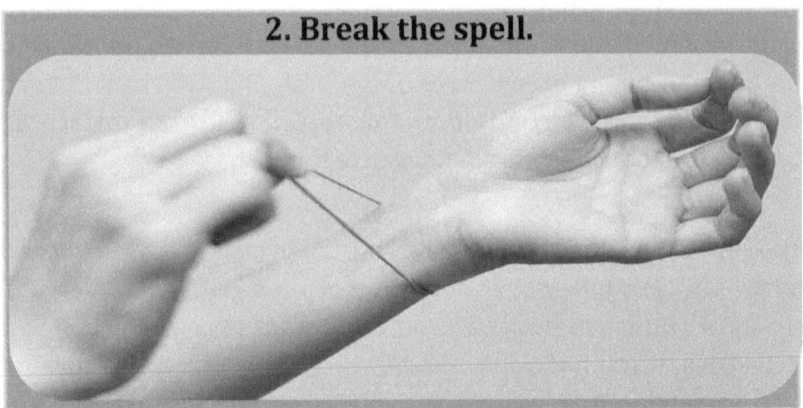

After you've spent two or three days noticing your thoughts and feelings, it's time to do something about them. Keep the rubber band on your wrist, and every time you notice negative thinking, gently pop the rubber band or move it to the other wrist. You want a physical pattern interrupt to break up the mental looping of negative thoughts. Then mentally identify and label what you were doing. "Oh, there's that negative thinking again. There are those thoughts and feelings popping up again." You want to dis-identify with the thoughts — they are separate from YOU as a person. It's important to recognize your thoughts as random products of consciousness instead of seeing them as reality.

3. Fill in the blank.

Once you interrupt the negative thought and identify it, you need to switch gears entirely. You can't leave a mental void, or you'll go directly back to negative thinking, which is an entrenched habit that's become natural for your brain. You must retrain your brain to think differently. So after you pop the rubber band, redirect your thoughts or actions. One way to do this is by reframing your thought to disprove it or make it positive. For example, if you're thinking, "I'll never get this project finished on time," then say to yourself, "No, that's not true. I can and will get it done on time. I always have in the past, and I will again." Even if you don't believe this totally, say it out loud or to yourself. Acknowledge any solid evidence you have that counters your negative thought.

Be rigorous in your efforts at redirecting your thoughts, just as you'd continue to put a toddler back in a time-out chair when they keep getting up. Eventually, your mind will know you mean business. You can also use positive action to replace negative thinking. If you find yourself ruminating over something unpleasant, get up and do something that will occupy your mind and distract you from your thoughts.

4. Practice daily gratitude.

With all of our negative thinking, sometimes it's hard to see how much is truly wonderful about our lives. To appreciate how great life really is, you must be intentional about it. I'd suggest keeping a gratitude journal, as writing tends to reinforce thinking. It's good to write in this journal at night before you go to bed, as you will fill your mind with positivity before you drift into sleep.

You may be in the midst of a crisis or worry, but that doesn't negate all of your many, many blessings. Write down each one in your journal, and as you write, really focus on the gratitude item and flood your mind with feelings of gratefulness.

Do this every day, even if you're repeating the same items over and over. This will help you keep gratitude at the forefront of your mind rather than in the dark recesses.

5. Stop reacting.

Small negative events during your day can trigger a cascade of pessimistic or angry thoughts and feelings. Someone says something rude to you. You comment back to them. They say something else. You go brood about it for hours. Traffic is bumper to bumper, and you're in a hurry. You honk your horn and feel your blood pressure rising. It takes you hours to calm down.

Every day life presents us with a multitude of dirty little tricks to goad us into negativity. But as the CEO of your mind, you can chose how you want to react. Sure, you can get pissed off, hurt, or frustrated — but you'll lose hours of your day that could be joyful. Instead, mindfully choose how you want to react. You know difficult things will happen on occasion, so mentally prepare. Teach yourself to take some deep, calming breaths.

Decide on a better way to respond that minimizes negativity. Acknowledge your knee-jerk reactions, but consciously decide not to follow them. If possible, try to find humor in the inanities and frustrations of life, as they are part of the human condition.

6. Find positive people.

We tend to absorb and reflect the emotions and attitudes of those we spend time with. If you're hanging around negative people who complain and worry much of the time, then you are bound to catch their ailment. You may need to make some hard decisions about who you spend time with, but if someone had a contagious disease, you'd have no trouble creating a boundary between you and them. Negativity is a contagious disease. Find people who uplift you and who are positive, happy, and confident. Do your best to spend less time with people who pull you down.

7. Have more fun.

We get so caught up in the serious business of life that we forget to simply have fun. When was the last time you played a game, rode a bike, flew a kite, or did anything carefree and non-competitive? We need daily fun to balance the stresses and demands of our complicated lives.

If you can't remember what feels fun to you, go back to your childhood and think about fun activities. I have a friend who swings on her children's swing set for relaxation and pleasure. Be vigilant in making fun part of your life.

8. Turn off the news.

Every time I watch the news, I feel worried and sad. A reporter might cover a story on a new health scare, and of course, I worry about that for myself. The never-ending coverage on terrorism, shootings, politics, and natural disasters makes us feel anxious and threatened.

Yes, there is plenty of bad news, and we need to stay informed. But there's plenty of good news as well. There are plenty of positive, happy, uplifting things going on in the world. So make a choice to limit the amount of news you watch, and instead find programs, podcasts, blogs, books, and articles that inspire and motivate you. Seek out positive information to fill your mind.

9. Simplify your life.

The busier and more complicated your life is, the more difficult it will be to remain positive. When you have too many demands and obligations, with little time for fun, reflection, relationships, or exercise, the more stressed and unhappy you are bound to feel.

We often resort to buying things to soothe our feelings, but all of these material things create stress as well, as you must store them, take care of them, and pay for them. Too much stuff drains your psychic energy. Simply the act of simplifying — dropping things from your to-do list and getting rid of stuff — will make you feel lighter and more positive.

Schedule a few days to streamline your life, giving yourself plenty of time and space for your most important life values and activities.

10. Spend time with friends and family.

Quality time spent with the people we love and cherish most is the best way to develop a positive attitude. People on their deathbeds report their biggest regret is not spending more time with friends and family.

Be proactive in making time for those you love. Initiate more family events, as well as one-on-one time with your spouse or partner, your children, and your friends. Create rituals and traditions that are meaningful and happy.
Mindfully choose to avoid family drama or conflict and speak words of love, affirmation, and healing to serve as an example and inspiration to others in your sphere.

There is how you can maintain a positive attitude all the time..!

1. Focusing on Your Present

Have you realized that most of the things that you tend to worry about for days at a stretch end up not taking place at all! Sometimes the things that you were so worried about were in fact not as big a problem as you thought it to be. So the key here is to focus all your attention on the present as much as possible. By doing so, you will be able to minimize the unnecessary fears and worries which eventually lead to negative emotions.

2. Speaking in a Positive Manner

Have you ever paid attention to how much of what you say is negative in nature? There are some individuals who have a habit of constantly complaining about anything such as weather, their work, their neighbors, their spouse, and so on. We all tend to do it occasionally. However, it is important to remind ourselves that our words are defined by our thoughts. So, the more you can look for positive things to say, the more positive your thoughts are likely to be. You must make it a compulsory habit to think only positive thoughts. If required, you must give yourself a small pep talk the first thing in the morning before you step out of your bed. You must understand that positive thinking is a habit. So it is very much possible to develop it once you learn how to do it with regular conscious practice.

3. Accepting Reality

It may be difficult initially to let go of your need for perfection and control in your life. However, it can be quite liberating once you learn to simply accept the reality that not always things will happen as per your desire and it is perfectly fine. When there are situations in life where things are not taking place as per your wishes, you must accept things the way they are, instead of wasting your energy on negative emotions. You must remember that it is the law of nature that most of the things pass with time.

4. Keeping Positive Company

It is a basic human nature that we have a habit to mimic the people with whom we spend most of our time with. As an example, observe how teenagers conform to the social code of their friends. It works in the same manner for everyone else as well. So, it all depends on the company that you mingle with. The more time you spend with people with a positive mindset, the more likely it is that you will start thinking and acting in a similar manner. Also, laughter is the best medicine. It is one of the wonderful ways to reduce stress and connect with ease with people around you. It generally makes you feel better all around.

5. Contributing Positively Towards Your Community

One of the ways in which you can feel more positive is to contribute positively towards your community in one way or the other. Whether you contribute your time, finances, or skills, it can be highly uplifting to help others. Apart from generating a good feeling, such thoughtful contribution makes a meaningful difference in someone's life. It also gives you a respite from your present problems and it even allows you to view your problems in a different light.

"I hope these 5 ways will definitely help you to maintain a positive attitude in life"

"Now it's time to stick with those three chapters '11', '12', '13' because these chapters are mostly followed by every billionaire in the word"

"Because working on your internal purity is the best path of success coz that the only way you can control your internal emotions to fight with any situation that comes in your way"

THERE ARE THOSE 3 SECRET WAY/CHAPPTER OF SUCCESS

1 *"Don't let discouragement stop you from pressing on"*

2 *"Be willing to work hard"*

3 *"Be brave enough to follow your intuition"*

{Let's talk in detail}

'Let's talk about the Eleventh chapter'

"Don't let discouragement stop you from pressing on"

11. DON'T LET DISCOURAGEMENT STOP YOU FROM PRESSING ON

I don't know where you are at this point in your life, but I am praying for you in advance that you don't become so discouraged to the point when you want to give up the fight. I want to encourage you today, "Don't do it!" Don't let discouragement stop you from being all that God wants you to be.

Trust me. I know that sometimes life can hit you hard, tests and trials come out of nowhere, and people can do or say things that will cause you to think and say, "Is it worth it?!" But I want to tell you, "Yes! It's worth it! Go through the pain. Go through the disappointments. Go through the fiery trials. Go through the harsh words." Because God has a plan for it all it's all a part of His will. It's all a part of your destiny. And most importantly, it's worth **heaven**.

The enemy brings discouragement when God is trying to do great things in our lives. And God allows it. Tests and trials are going to come, but know that they are meant to make us stronger in character and train us to be more effective for advancing the kingdom of heaven. James 1:2-4 says, "Dear brothers and sisters, whenever trouble comes your way, let it be an opportunity for joy. For when your faith is tested, your endurance has a chance to grow. So let it grow, for when your endurance is fully developed, you will be strong in character and ready for anything." (NLT) *Meditate on this one!*

Jesus also tells us in John 16:33, "...Here on earth you will have many trials and sorrows. But take heart, because I have overcome the world." Know that Jesus sees the big picture, we only see in part. So even though we must go through tough things in this life, it's great to know that through Christ we are victorious, and we're not alone in the process.

I want to share something that happened to me once. And I'm going to be pretty transparent...

One evening, I became very discouraged. It was something that someone had said to me that was pretty discouraging and harsh. It actually hurt me to the point that caused me to question the promises of God for my life. And I'd never been there before. But it happened. I was *officially* discouraged.

So I cried out to God about it. I told him where I was, and that it hurt. Sure, I knew the Scriptures, but at that particular time, I was slowly allowing the enemy to weigh me down with doubt, because of what someone else had told me.

After I cried out to Him, I climbed into bed and fell asleep and the Lord gave me a dream that night. He gave me a dream where I was attacked by a barrage of fireballs. But as I ran through this courtyard to dodge each one, none of them touched me. And as I ran, Isaiah 43:2 rose up inside of me that says, "...When you walk through the fire of oppression, you will not be burned up; the flames will not consume you." And shortly thereafter, I woke up. *I'll never forget that dream.* **And I'll never forget that verse.**

The next day, I asked my husband if he wouldn't mind if I took a ride. He was okay with it. So I took a long drive and talked to God about what was happening in my life. And when I got to Barnes & Noble to do my devotion, the Lord led me to a book entitled, "Taking Your Life Back One Thought at a Time...Letting Go of Your Past, Enjoying Your Present, and Looking Forward to the Future," by Annie Chapman. This book was life-changing!

I realized that day, that the battle was in my mind. I was allowing the enemy to wage war there. That day in Barnes & Noble was what I call, "A God-moment"! As I spent the day in that bookstore, the Lord met me in my personal devotion, through His Word, a new book, and He helped me to encourage myself in Him, while forgiving the person who had hurt me.

By the time I packed up to leave, I felt like a weight had been lifted. I was strengthened and ENCOURAGED! My joy was restored! And it wasn't that my circumstance had changed. But it was more about my mind being renewed. God led me on a pathway to overcoming *discouragement*. And now I know what it feels like to be discouraged. And that's why I'm writing to you about this today.

Again, I know what it feels like to be discouraged. I know what it feels like when it seems like you just can't take another step or another beating in this spiritual fight. But I want to encourage you today to encourage yourself in the Lord. Speak His Word over your situation. And cry out to Him. And when you do, He will be there to help you. I know it.

I'll encourage you as I encourage myself with these words..."Hold onto God's promises. Guard your mind and your heart in these last days. Don't grow weary in well doing, because in due season, you will reap, if you faint not. And lastly, don't let discouragement stop you."

Remember, Jesus is coming back soon! And those who endure unto the end shall be saved. So let's be ready from the *Inside Out.*

There are five best ways to don't let discouragement stop you from pressing on

1. **Be honest.**

It does you no good to pretend you don't feel what you feel. You can't take action against a negative feeling until you first admit you have it. A strong Christian is not someone who never experiences negative feelings. It's someone who has learned what to do with them when he or she has them and how to process them biblically.

2. Take care of your body.

If your body isn't working, your mind, emotions and will are also weakened. I love how God tended to Elijah's body first—before addressing anything else and provided ravens to feed him. Sometimes the circumstances of life drain us dry, and we need to press pause, stop doing, and simply rest and refresh.

3. Pay attention to your thought life.

Maturing as believers means we learn to think truthfully (Philippians 4:8) and to take every thought captive to the obedience of Christ (2 Corinthians 10:5).

All of us attempt to make sense of the things that happen in our lives. We try to figure out why they happen and what it all means. It's crucial that we pay attention to what stories we are telling ourselves about ourselves, about others, about God or a particular situation, and whether or not those stories are actually true. For example, if you look at what Elijah was telling himself after he became discouraged, much of it was not true, yet because he thought it, it added to his misery (read 1 Kings 19).

Jeremiah was also telling himself things about God that were not true but because his mind believed his version of reality instead of God's, he lost his hope. Read through Lamentations 3. Notice in verse 21 Jeremiah begins to have a change of mind and heart. He says, "This I recall to mind, therefore I have hope." When his thoughts changed his negative emotions also lifted even though his circumstances stayed the same.

4. Train yourself to see life out of two lenses at the same time.

When the apostle Paul counsels us to be transformed by the renewing of our mind (Romans 12:2), he is telling us that our mind needs to be trained to think differently than we have in the past. Part of this training is to learn to see both the temporal (life is hard) and the eternal (God has a purpose here) at the same time.

Paul speaks honestly of his temporal pain when he says he is hard pressed on every side, perplexed, persecuted and struck down. Yet he did not become crushed, despairing, abandoned, or destroyed. Why not? Because he learned to firmly fix the eternal perspective on his spiritual eyes. He says, "Therefore we do not lose heart…. So we fix our eyes not on what is seen, but on what is unseen. For what is seen is temporary, but what is unseen is eternal" (2 Corinthians 4:8-18).

Paul never minimized the pain of the temporal, yet discouragement didn't win because he knew that God's purposes were at work. (See Philippians 1:12 –14 for another example).

5. Press close into God

The truth is life is hard, people do disappoint and hurt us, and we don't always understand God or his ways. The prophet Nahum talks about a day of trouble and reminds us "The Lord is good, *a stronghold in the day of trouble*, he knows those who trust in him" (Nahum 1:7). If we're not in close trusting relationship with God, life's troubles can become unbearable. The psalmist cried out, "I would have despaired *unless* I had believed I would see God in the land of the living" (Psalm 27).

One final tip the best way to chase out a negative feeling is with another feeling. The Bible teaches us "In everything give thanks for this is the will of God" (1 Thessalonians 5:18). Gratitude is a powerful anecdote for discouragement. We may not be able to give God thanks for the difficult situation that we find ourselves in, but we can learn to look for things we can be thankful for in the midst of it.

Now it's time to move on another chapter

'Let's talk about the Twelfth chapter'

"Be willing to work hard"

12. BE WILLING TO WORK HARD

This is a true story of my close neighbor

When I was in middle school I started to play football for my school. I had never played tackle football but was raised in a family that was obsessed with football.

This put a lot of pressure on me. I wanted to succeed and be able to play at a high level to help my team, but I was unsure if I would be good enough to even compete.

At the time this gave me an inner drive that helped me quite a bit. Because I felt behind the others I chose to work harder. I would be the first one to finish my warm-up lap and would also jump into any situation to gain as much experience as I could.

This strategy paid off. I was open to learning so I took instruction from the coaches very well. Because of this effort I ended up winning an award that was given every year to the person who exemplified the work ethic of a former player who passed away in a tragic accident. Since I had grown up with this individual, receiving an award in his honor meant a great deal to me.

But this positive feedback started to get to my head. I thought that I had enough talent that meant I didn't have to work as hard. For a year or so those hard work habits continued but they soon disintegrated and were replaced with an elevated ego that kept me from giving my best all the time.

By the end of my high school football career I stopped working hard. It wasn't just with football. I started to take the mindset that I could get around the hard work by being more talented or finding some secret way around a problem etc.

I went through this pattern in several other areas of my life as well. Looking at it at a high level I basically would start feeling somewhat insecure and use hard work and a willingness to learn. This would give me an incredible advantage.

Then slowly I would feel more and more entitled. I would feel I was owed more than I received and would turn bitter. This bitterness would result in slacking off and being close-minded. This would result in me getting further and further away from the hard work and open-minded approach that is needed.

Once I started to realize this pattern I finally was able to address it and correct it. I started to realize that if I started focusing on what was *owed* to me I would lose sight of what *I* needed to *do* to keep having success.

It sounds easy but it was several times going through this pattern before I was able to change how I responded. Several jobs followed this pattern and started great but ended poorly due to my ego getting too big and feeling I was owed more than what I was receiving.

I started to realize that if we avoid trying to determine what we deserve, and keep our focus on all that we receive, we are much more willing to keep working and keep an open mind.

Now when I start to feel this entitled attitude coming on, I do everything I can to shift that mindset. Instead of feeling entitled, I keep working and do everything possible to keep an open mind. I don't know everything and many times I overlook certain elements in my attempt to justify my entitlement.

If you find yourself in this cycle, stop for a minute and think about how your focus shifts. Instead of focusing on doing everything possible to succeed we shift to focusing on external things that we don't like.

As soon as this starts to be the focus, stop and commit to doing the work. Keep working through it and do everything possible to change your mind set. Think of Maya Angelou's quote, *"Nothing will work unless you do."*

This entitlement mindset can be defeated but it takes hard work and a shift back to focusing on what we can do to improve, not on external forces that we don't like. Keep working through this cycle until you can start to change the pattern.

THERE ARE FIVE BEST WAYS TO BE WILLING TO WORK HARD

1. Get clear on the end goal

The trick to keeping your motivation up through low points and exhausted periods, traveler Marie Stein insists, isn't any particular productivity technique or energy-boosting idea; rather, it's being really, really clear about why you're doing what you doing.

"There is only one way for me to motivate myself to work hard: I don't think about it as hard work. I think about it as part of making myself into who I want to be," she writes. "The 'hard' part for me is choosing and accepting what it is that I have to do... Once I've made the choice to do something, I try not to think so much about how difficult or frustrating or impossible that might be; I just think about how good it must feel to be that, or how proud I might be to have done that."

Struggling to keep your focus on that end vision? "Just ask yourself: If you were the person that you want to be, then what would that person do?" suggests student Karl Bradley Saclolo.

2. Take care of yourself physically

Sometimes the problem isn't mental, it's physical. Your willpower can be at an all-time high, but if you don't have the physical energy to complete your work, keeping your motivation up is still going to be difficult.

"Are you tired a lot? Do you get enough sleep? Do you experience some constant unpleasantness, such as poor sinuses or a constant pain? Are you sad or upset or just lethargic all the time for no reason you can pinpoint?" asks freelance writer April Gunn. If so, "get to a doctor if you can for a routine physical, just to make sure everything is working properly. Try your best to get seven to nine hours of sleep a night. Listen to your body when it's telling you things, seek out the causes of your discomfort, and deal with them as best you can.

"It's really hard to get and stay motivated to work hard if you're not feeling your best," she concludes.

3. Think habits, not motivation

Getting yourself to do something again and again by sheer force of will is extremely difficult. Getting yourself to do something by force of habit is easier. "Because motivation/willpower is a limited resource, it has helped me to instead build habits which, once instilled, don't use willpower," explains entrepreneur Bud Hennekes. "Start with small habits that help you be more productive and make you feel good. For example, you could aim to walk 15 minutes a day or work in short bursts of intense focus."

Entrepreneur James Clear has endorsed this advice on Inc.com, though he frames it a bit differently. Rather than habits, he talks about the power of "schedules," but whichever term you use, the effect is the same--automating a behavior by integrating it into your routine means you rely less on willpower

4. Embrace discomfort

Manager Mart Nijland suggests that those struggling with motivation remember the wisdom of bodybuilders: no pain, no gain. It is a cliche, but there's no way to expand your abilities without going outside your comfort zone, so stop letting a little bit of unpleasantness sap your motivation. In fact, struggling a little is a good sign.

"For anything you want to work harder for, you have to go beyond that threshold," he writes, "because you grow into a totally different, much stronger person."

5. Bribe (or punish) yourself

Not all routes to improved motivation are high-minded. One of the more effective ways will also motivate your dog--simple reward and punishment. "Make yourself an offer that you can't refuse," suggests analyst Deepak Singh (but don't go as far as Don Corleone, please).

Both positive and negative incentives can work. "For example, if you want to read a book, set a deadline and a reward. Say, if you love ice cream, you could eat some as soon as you finish the book," suggests Singh. It might not sound very grand, but pushing yourself to complete a task by dangling treats (or the threat of public humiliation or a pay-out on a bet with a friend) appears to be effective.

Now it's time to move on another chapter

'Let's talk about the thirteenth chapter'

"Be brave enough to follow your intuition"

13. BE BRAVE ENOUGH TO FOLLOW YOUR INTUITION

Be brave enough to trust your intuition and listen to your heart...it truly knows everything! Follow your heart and pursue what gives you the greatest and deepest sense of joy, love and fulfillment because at the end of the day that is your mission and purpose during this life time! If you are feeling lost, feeling down or even uncertain that is a sign that you haven't been listening to your heart and expressing yourself and sharing your beauty and potential with the world and maybe it's time to trust yourself and listen to your own heart and follow your dreams! Don't waste another minute on this planet doing something or being something that doesn't make your heart and soul feel a deep sense of joy, love, fulfillment and purpose!

Do you believe in your intuition? Many of us 'go with our gut' when we make quick decisions While intuition may seem somewhat mystical, it's really our hunches formed using past knowledge and experiences. Does intuition have a place in the business world? Many would say no, but can you train your gut instinct to serve you better? Steve Jobs, who was known for being the co-founder and CEO of Apple, passed away several years ago. But he left behind a rich legacy of innovation and imagination. His work as a businessman and as an inventor changed our modern world.

USING INTUITION TO CHANGE THE WORLD

Jobs spent seven months in India, and he felt that his sense of intuition was influenced by people that he met and studied with. Zen meditation had a profound impact on young Jobs, and future designs of the iPhone reflected his appreciation for simplicity.

While there was nothing magical about Steve Jobs, his ideas were certainly revolutionary. He was able to reinvent his company and adapt his vision with agility. He trusted his instincts, and he was able to play a significant role in developing modern hand-held electronic devices.

"Have the courage to follow your heart and intuition."

Like he did (Steve Jobs)

To be intuitive, you need to be self-aware and connected to everything that is happening around you. You need to listen to your body and mind and understand how you interact with your environment.

PEOPLE MAY BE SKEPTICAL, AND THAT'S ALRIGHT

People may not accept intuition as easily as a rational explanation. If you are able to show results, however, they may be more inclined to let you trust your instincts. Being intuitive doesn't mean that you will be right all the time, it just means accessing a little bit of extra information that you can use to make a more sounded decision.

THERE ARE SOME GREAT WAYS THAT HELP YOU TO BE BRAVE ENOUGH TO FOLLOW YOUR INTUITION

1.

Notice where you hear or feel the fear in your body

Intuition comes as a gut felling or instinct. You'll feel it deep in your belly with a sense of inner knowing. Oftentimes, this intuitive guidance is more of a felling than a thought. It may just be a sensation more than words, or there may be one or two really direct words like stop no or don't do it. Even if you don't hear words from your intuition, you just know it because you can feel it clearly in your gut. (Some people even say that their intuition has been so strong in their bodies that it physically moves them)

The fears that come from your mind are heard in your head. Rather than felt in your body. These fears appear as a voice with a lot of stuff to say. The voice will ramble on endlessly with worries and assumptions, imagining the worst of outcomes and getting really ridiculously negative. This fear is a waste of energy, and it's best to ignore it. I recommend taking some deep breaths, going for a walk, listening to music or journaling in order to get these crazy thoughts out and let them go.

"A sure sign that the fear is just in your mind is that it passes within a day or even a couple of hours! Intuitive fear is firm, direct, and steady"

2.

Try the A or B Test

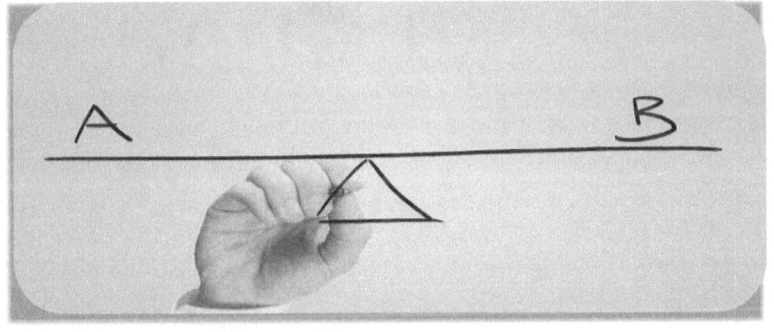

Imagine that you're stressed out with making a big decision. You want to be brave but you're not sure which choice is the best for you. Which fear is real? Which fear is a setback?

In this situation, try A or B test Imagine that you could ask the advice of some you really respect and love: should you do A or B?

And imagine that this person responds, Definitely A, without a doubt."Then feel what happen in your body"

If you get a sinking, sick felling in your gut, that's your intuition saying, "Nope! Don't listen to them!"

But if you feel suddenly energized, open and excited that's your intuition saying, "Woohoo" that's the answer I really wanted hear! You know that choice is best for you, based on your intuition.

3.

Practice asking your intuition a question

Once you've figured out what these different gut felling are like (big yes or big no from your intuition), practice asking your intuition different question to test this out.

The keys here are that you first calm your mind, and then be very patient with the answer.

I remember closing your eyes and taking a few deep breaths. Let yourself relax for a moment. Calm down your mind by becoming very aware of your body and how it feels (try meditation to help you relax before doing this exercise!)

When you feel ready, ask your intuition a yes or no question and then wait. Observe how your gut feels. Notice if your mind starting answering the question right away.

Try to be patient and wait for that inner-knowing felling or perhaps a few direct words of advice.

Have fun with this! Don't get discouraged if you find it difficult at first to keep your mind out of the way. It just takes practice.

And remember-the answer is not always what it to be, but you'll fell in your body that it's right.

NOW IT'S YOU'RE TIME TO DO SOMTHIMG THAT YOU WANT TO DO, BECAUSE THE WORLD IS A JUNGLE, YOU EITHER FIGHT AND DOMINATE, OR HIDE AND EVAPORATE IT'S TOTALLY UP OT YOU.

I hope these ways' / tips whatever you call it will help you to make your life happy, healthy and successful.

Had back with another motivation book soon

If that book is helpful for you so please share our book with your friends and family; If you want a another motivation book so, please write your requirements in review we will definitely work on it so don't be hesitate for writing a reviews...!

The end..!

www.ingramcontent.com/pod-product-compliance
Lightning Source LLC
Chambersburg PA
CBHW030643220526
45463CB00004B/1623